The Dream of Lafcadio Hearn

Roger Pulvers

The Dream of Lafcadio Hearn

Roger Pulvers

Kurodahan Press
2011

The Dream of Lafcadio Hearn

Roger Pulvers

Copyright © 2011 Roger Pulvers

This edition copyright © 2011 Kurodahan Press. All rights reserved. No part of this publication may be reproduced in whole or in part, or stored in a retrieval system, or transmitted in any form or by any means, electronic, mechanical, photocopying, recording, or otherwise, without written permission from the publisher.

FG-JP0031-L37

ISBN-13: 978-4-902075-41-0

ISBN-10: 4-902075-41-5

KURODAHAN PRESS

Kurodahan Press is a division of Intercom, Ltd.

#403 Tenjin 3-9-10, Chuo-ku, Fukuoka 810-0001 JAPAN

www.kurodahan.com

*For Susan
and our children—
Jeremy, Alice, Sophie and Lucy*

Contents

The Life of Lafcadio Hearn..................... ix
Foreword....................................... 3
1890–1891   Matsue 5
1894–1895   Kobe 89
1904   Tokyo 131
Afterword 185
About the author 187
About the cover............................. 189

The Life of Lafcadio Hearn

He created an illusion and lived his days and nights within its confines. That illusion was his Japan. He found in Japan the ideal coupling of the cerebral and the sensual, the one constantly recharging the other and catalyzing in him the inspiration to write.

He came at a time when virtually all foreigners were in Japan to instruct, pontificate or lord themselves over the Oriental upstart; yet he himself was in Japan to learn, to scavenge, to discover what his temperament had taught him was beautiful, potent and bizarre in the human spirit. Fresh off the ship in 1890, he wrote of the Japanese to his friend and subsequent biographer Elizabeth Bisland, "I believe that their art is as far in advance of our art as old Greek art was superior to that of the earliest European art-groupings. We are barbarians! I do not merely think these things: I am as sure of them as of death. I only wish I could be reincarnated in some little Japanese baby, so that I could see and feel the world as beautifully as a Japanese brain does."

It was hard for Japanese to resist such blatant adoration, focused as they were on their sheer uniqueness, though it took them some time to acknowledge his contribution to the notion of that uniqueness.

More than 160 years have passed since the birth of Lafcadio Hearn. This orphan of Europe found in Japan what he had been seeking everywhere: a sanctuary for his imagination. In the decades following his death in Tokyo in 1904, the Japanese crowned him with their ultimate laurel: He became their "Gaijin Laureate," the single greatest non-native interpreter, in their eyes, of their inmost cultural secrets. Even today, Hearn is considered in this country the foreigner who understood the Japanese in the most profound way. Yet he is largely forgotten in the West, a footnote on the faded pages of exotica.

What was the nature of this man, a misfit and wanderer, a non-native informant of the fiendish details of American and Japanese lore? (Hearn was a chronicler of American mores as well as of Japanese.) What were the circumstances that led to such a gap between Japanese and Western perceptions of this dutifully forlorn eccentric?

There were many factors that allowed Hearn to feel immediately at home in Meiji Japan, stemming as much from the circumstances of his birth in Greece, his early years of education in Ireland and England, and his period of newspaper apprenticeship in America as from the peculiar realities of Japan at the end of the nineteenth century, a country in the throes of grossly accelerated progress. He was a man abandoned by family, a man who had never felt a part of a social entity anywhere, a man so intensely withdrawn that he had, at times, preferred the company of a corpse in the morgue to that of a living human. He found in Japan the one thing that had eluded him entirely in his life up till then: respect for him as an individual . . . though, paradoxically, he rejected the basis of that respect shown him by the Japanese, namely his birthright.

In Dublin, he had been a little dark boy left by his parents to be reared by a pious great-aunt. In England, he had been a sensitive, short-statured adolescent, as different a type as you could get in the County Durham countryside, thrown on the mercies of dogmatic martinet teachers. In London, he had been miserably down and out, a scavenger in the markets, a young man absolutely isolated, terrified by the squalor that seemed always to be on the verge of engulfing him. Half-Irish and half-Greek, in both appearance and disposition very much *not* the Englishman, he was lost in location and, what would prove to be more telling, in time.

Then, suddenly, there was America, at age nineteen, where he found his way to Cincinnati and a job at a newspaper. He styled himself into a reporter, but hardly the kind that the country wished to nurture—fit, perhaps, for writing police reports, a scandal chaser, a grubber on the Rue Morgue, not at all your "go West, young man" type. Here, and later in New Orleans, he lived often in rooms that also accommodated blacks. He was of their class there, and he did not entertain the prejudices toward people of color that virtually all white Americans harbored. In fact, he was no doubt bundled in with "the inferior races" in the eyes of many of the good white people of post-Civil War America.

Post-Civil War America may have been steeped in the rhetoric of a theoretical egalitarian ideal, but, in reality, little had changed for the non-white population of either North or South. Hearn, with his olive skin, identified with color. This alone marginalized him in his chosen field of journalism. Americans were themselves, like the Japanese of the Meiji era, on a journey of self-discovery. In an America that was forging a cultural identity separate from Europe's—just as Japan was forging an identity separate from the rest of Asia's—how could there be a place for a man of such incongruous cultural predilections, one with a downward, not an upward, gaze? Hearn was an anti-elitist in a country with an elite dominated by white Anglo-Saxon Protestants.

Hearn was drawn south to New Orleans, to what he saw as a languid and decadent lifestyle. A refuge for the defeated spirit, the South proved to be a place where Hearn, cultural underdog himself, could lick his wounds with the best of them. Eventually, he was tempted to travel still farther south, to Saint-Pierre on the island of Martinique, which he called "nude, warm, savage, amorous." (Hearn, a powerful swimmer, greatly enjoyed swimming in the lake by Mount Pelée at the northern tip of the island.)

Roger Pulvers

He didn't settle in Saint-Pierre. He missed the intellectual life of the north. Hearn was, after all, a fanatic bookworm and self-proclaimed polemicist. He was no Paul Gauguin. The torpid pace of life in the tropics—particularly the Francophone tropics where he felt in danger of losing his command of English style—was not, in the end, the cup of tea of a man with a hyperactive mind.

In Saint-Pierre, and again after he returned to New Orleans, he fell seriously ill with a fever that must have weakened his heart and led, eventually, to his death. Reporting work had all but evaporated. Hearn's relations with his publishers in New York seemed tenuous at best. In 1879, he opened a restaurant with a partner. (Hearn's interest in food was deep and abiding. A Creole cookbook compiled, written and illustrated by him is once again in print today, though at the time of publication he refused to have his name on the cover lest it brand him as a "cookbook author.") In fact, his greatest nostalgia of all, during the years he forfeited his tastes to a bland Japanese diet, might have been for the pungent food of New Orleans. He had put up $100, a good two months' salary, but his partner ran off with cash and cook, leaving Hearn holding the pot in the defunct eatery that he had named, prophetically, "The Hard Times."

And then came the windfall . . . and Hearn found himself on a ship bound from Vancouver, British Columbia, for, of all places, Japan. Looking back on Hearn's life, it is clear that he reinvented himself at this point in his life, from his first days in Japan. He was now in a country that looked up to someone from the "civilized" West. None of the prejudice that he had borne the brunt of for his mixed ancestry and out-of-the-ordinary looks would be in evidence in Meiji Japan. And it wasn't long before a new, enhanced individual was born: the single-minded connoisseur of things Japanese. In Japan, he came into his own.

Would Lafcadio Hearn's career as an author of fiction have taken flight had he remained in the United States? A short novel that he wrote while on Martinique, *Youma*, garnered an immense fee when it was serialized in *Harper's Magazine* in early 1890. But, a reading of this and his other fiction today reveals the sad truth that Lafcadio Hearn's prose is often purplish and lacking in originality. His works of fiction are of interest now primarily for the strangeness of their locations.

But Hearn was a story *re*teller of genius, a writer with an instinctive knack for grasping the essence of foreign cultures' spirituality, legends, rituals and myths. The underlying reason for this, I feel, is his personal, if subconscious, refusal to identify with the Anglo-Celtic cultures of his youth and early manhood. Hearn represented no country in an era when authors were seen as conduits for their countries' souls. The Japanese may believe that he identified with Japan to the extent that he "became" Japanese in his own mind, but that was not the case either. He was prepared to give a voice to any culture that was not associated with Western institutions of church or state. The tendency among some Japanese and non-Japanese scholars and journalists to emphasize Hearn's Greek or Irish roots, as if these were anything more than nationalities inherited from parents he barely knew, misleads one in the judgment of the man's true nature and disposition.

He came to Japan at a time when the Japanese were eagerly embracing the West in all its industrial and imperialistic trappings (although rejecting its monotheistic religion). This gives rise to the essential paradox of Lafcadio Hearn: He became the interpreter of a Japanese soul that the Japanese themselves were loath to expose or recognize until, once safely modernized, they could take it up again and rediscover him as the emperor of their bruised nostalgia.

Lafcadio Hearn was born on June 27, 1850 on the Greek island of Lefkas, one of the Ionian Islands that were, from 1815 until 1864, occupied by the British Imperial Army Protectorate Forces. His father, Charles Bush Hearn, a staff surgeon in the British Army, was stationed temporarily on the island. Hearn's mother was Rosa Kassimati, originally of Kythera. Hearn's elder brother, George, died at age one, not two months after Hearn's birth; and with Charles off at sea, the trauma for Rosa must have been considerable. The Hearn family of Dublin were well-to-do Protestant Irish, and it was to that city that Lafcadio was taken by his mother in 1852, when he was two years old.

Charles was soon dispatched to the West Indies, then later to the Crimea; and the couple eventually divorced . . . or, more precisely, the marriage was annulled on the grounds that Rosa had not signed the marriage certificate. Being functionally illiterate, needless to say, she hadn't been able to. It is clear from recollections of Hearn's relatives in Dublin that Rosa suffered from rather severe depression. One can imagine this woman, a native of Lefkas, the "Jewel of the Ionian Islands," latitude 38 degrees, accustomed to warm sunny skies, thrust into the gloomy and damp atmosphere of Dublin, located a full 15 degrees north.

Ireland was just emerging, when she arrived there, from the Great Famine. Though the country had lost approximately one-quarter of its population through death and emigration, the population of Dublin had actually increased during the famine years of 1845–1852. Rosa, whose command of English was apparently minimal, must have suffered greatly. She returned to Greece pregnant, giving birth to another boy, James, in her home country in August 1854. Lafcadio never saw her again and never met his brother. (James, who emigrated to the United States in 1871, just two years after his elder brother, made an attempt to meet up with him, but the latter refused to see him.)

With no clear recollection of his mother and only fragments of memory of his father, who visited him in Dublin when he was little, Lafcadio was brought up by his great-aunt Sarah Brenane. She was a fervent convert to Catholicism, living in Rathmines, then and now a fashionable district of Dublin. She sent him off to a Catholic school in France, though it is unclear where exactly in France this was, and in 1863 to Ushaw College (also called St. Cuthbert's College), a Roman Catholic school in County Durham, northeast England, where he remained until he was seventeen. It was there that Hearn lost his sight in one eye, apparently in a game called "Giant's Stride," in which a stick is swung on a

The Life of Lafcadio Hearn

rope around a pole. Whether this was a true accident, one cannot know. It was also at school in England that Hearn started to build his muscles, a defense against the isolation and estrangement he increasingly felt. Hearn's mistrust of the church and disdain for missionaries that were to become so blatant in Japan no doubt had their origins here and at his Catholic school in France.

At school in England, where he was deeply unhappy, he endured, in addition to the austere and doctrinaire training by stern schoolmasters, the most conventional bullying by his peers. That "Paddy" (as Irish males were wont to be called by the English) took refuge in two things that would later stand him in good stead was understandable, those two things being his physical prowess and his refractive imagination. As an adult, he stood just 160 cm high, but his well-developed muscles, timidity's armor, protected him. He was painfully introverted, and the deforming loss of sight in one eye only exacerbated his shyness. In particular, he came to feel that no woman of his own kind would look favorably on him, with his exophthalmic stare and his gloomy perception of the twisted realities of human nature.

After his great-aunt fell on hard times, Hearn was forced to leave school and travel to London, where he lived for a time with a maid who had once worked in the Dublin household. He detested London with a passion all his life, having experienced there only extreme indigence. Then, when he was nineteen, came the opportunity to go to America. He was sent away, actually fobbed off. By now his great-aunt was virtually destitute and could no longer cope with the burden of looking after her ward. She passed away two years later, in 1871.

The nineteen-year-old Hearn arrived in New York and made his way to Cincinnati, Ohio, where he sank easily to the bottom of the melting pot. But, in multiracial Cincinnati, Hearn was ambitious to find a niche for himself. He was taken in by a printer, Henry Watkin, and taught typesetting; and in the autumn of 1872 began to write regular freelance articles for the *Enquirer*.

Due to a liaison in 1874 with a woman of mixed blood—Alethea Foley, a single mother at the time—he was fired from the paper. (The owner and publisher of the *Enquirer*, Washington McLean, was an unreconstructed sympathizer of the Southern cause. Incidentally, the McLean family also owned the *Washington Post*.) Although Lafcadio and Alethea did hold a wedding ceremony, interracial marriage was illegal in Ohio at the time. To disregard the propriety of the day in such a flamboyant way was seen by those in Hearn's white milieu as an outrageous and despicable act. It was not likely that Hearn, due to his background and status, could contemplate marriage to a "respectable" white woman; and, in any case, he passed most of his time with people who would now be called slum dwellers.

Hearn's outlook on the misery of the blacks and of people of mixed background is often very moving. In "Story of a Slave," published in the *Cincinnati Commercial* on April 2, 1876, Hearn tells the tragic story of Henrietta Woods, a black slave who was freed and then enslaved again by unscrupulous traders. "Story of a Slave," with its documentary-style descriptions of the plight of the blacks before and after the Civil War, is, to my mind, as good as any short work of Langston Hughes or Ralph Ellison. Thanks to the fact that he saw himself as representing no country or culture, Hearn was able to empathize with the blacks, as he did with the Japanese from the moment he set foot on Japanese soil. He did not judge others as "lower" because they did not live up to a presumed standard of culture, which he, in any case, rejected.

Hearn had a way of arriving in a place when it was in decline (with the exception of Japan, of course). Cincinnati had once been a thriving city, thanks to its strategic location on the north bank of the Ohio River, with thousands of steamboats stopping at its docks. At one time it was America's largest and wealthiest inland city, called in 1854 by Henry Wadsworth Longfellow "the Queen of the West/In her garlands dressed/On the banks of the Beautiful River." The location on the northern edge of the South and the southern edge of the North had played well . . . until two things changed the city's prosperous course: the Civil War and Chicago.

Chicago, the upstart, always saw Cincinnati as the town to beat. When the latter started up a professional baseball team, the Red Stockings, the former answered with the White Stockings. Cincinnati had been the pork-packing capital of America. Chicago took its place. The vehicle that powered Chicago's rise to power was the railroad. Cincinnati had always been one the gateways to the West, but after the Gold Rush in California, Chicago, with its rail link, stole the gate and everything that went with it.

Hearn wallowed in Cincinnati lowlife, particularly that centered around the levee. Hearn himself was feisty and passionate, and he spent many evenings with the stevedores—two-thirds of whom were black—the tramps, and the roustabouts of the dockland. He immersed himself in the lurid and gritty subculture of America for the first time, eventually writing about it in hundreds of articles. He covered the opium den, the brothel and the slaughterhouse, among other unsavory locales.

It is his ethnographic approach to reportage that, I believe, schooled him in his later studies of Japanese folklore. The culture of Meiji Japan was decidedly Western-oriented, but the subculture was still rooted in the mores, superstitions, rituals, and folklore of the Edo period and earlier. Without his American apprenticeship in the documenting of subculture, Hearn would have been just another Western-biased analyzer of and facile commentator on Japanese life.

Some of his best writing on the folklore of Cincinnati's subculture focuses on music and language. Here are portraits of blacks loving, talking, dancing, singing and "slapping juba." (Slapping, or patting, juba was a method of creating a drum beat by using spoons, washboards, or the person's own chest and legs. The use of drums had been banned on plantations in the South.) Whether recording the romantic words of "The Wandering Steamboat Man" or the vibrant rhythms of the levee culture, Hearn was a faithful chronicler of the life of a cityscape all but invisible to the city's well-to-do citizens.

Hearn was locally acclaimed for his reporting of crimes and scandals. His imagination was ignited by the kind of demonic detail that newspaper readers begged for then, as they do now. But in Cincinnati he was active on what was, at the time, the fringe of American culture. Ohio had been the West. The term "Middle West" did not gain currency until the end of the nineteenth century. But the defeat of the South had sent refugees to Chicago, giving prominence to that city as a new center of commerce. In addition, the Gold Rush had triggered massive emigration to California, which, now a state of the Union, was establishing itself as the new western frontier.

Here is an example of Hearn's reportage from his Cincinnati days:

> On lifting the coffin lid a powerful and penetrating odor, strongly resembling the smell of burnt beef, yet heavier and fouler, filled the room. Laid upon the clean white lining of the coffin [the remains] resembled great shapeless lumps of half-burnt bituminous coal . . . masses of crumbling human bones strung together by half-burnt sinews or glued one upon another by a hideous adhesion of half-molten flesh, boiled brains and jellied blood. The skull had burst like a shell in the fierce furnace heat; and the whole upper portion seemed as though it had been blown out by the steam from the boiling and bubbling brains.

This is an excerpt from Lafcadio Hearn's article, "Violent Cremation," from *The Cincinnati Enquirer* of November 9, 1874. In fact, this very long piece persists in grisly descriptions, such as of "a roasted liver and kidneys fairly fried," dealing with the so-called Tanyard Murder. The body belonged to the victim of a murder-by-cremation, and Hearn speculates that the poor man may very well have been alive when flung into the furnace. (The fellow had been incinerated by the father of the 15-year-old girl who had been made pregnant by him.)

The Life of Lafcadio Hearn

In another article, this one titled "Gibbeted," from the *Cincinnati Commercial* of August 26, 1876, Hearn takes up the execution of James Murphy, the nineteen-year-old son of Irish immigrants. In what I believe to be one of Hearn's best pieces of writing from any period, he describes in even tones "the pyramid of agony" confronting the lad after Father Murphy (no relation), "a fat, kindly, red-cheeked Irish priest," tried to comfort the boy on his way to the gallows.

Hearn is there to witness the event. The first attempt to gibbet the boy fails. There is a "pitiful groan" from the boy beneath his black hood.

"Why, I ain't dead. I ain't dead!"

Father Murphy inquires: "Are you hurt, my child?"

"No, father, I'm not dead. I'm not hurt. What are they going to do with me?"

The executioners then take the "ghastly mask" off the boy's head to fasten a new noose to his neck.

"His face was livid, his limbs shook with terror, and he suddenly seized Deputy Freeman desperately by the coat, saying in a husky whisper, 'What are you going to do with me?'"

"Then the little Irish priest whispered firmly in his ear, 'Let go, my son; let go, like a man—be a man; die like a man.'"

Hearn goes on to depict the young man's agonizingly slow (17-minute) death in painstaking and gruesome detail.

Here is nineteenth-century journalism at its wordy best—matter-of-fact, steely-eyed description. A good deal of the reportage that Lafcadio Hearn did in Cincinnati was perceptive and composed. It foreshadows his fastidious investigative approach to the esoterica of Japanese traditions.

Hearn's haunt in Cincinnati was the so-called Dead Man's Corner, his fellow travelers the derelicts and shady wheeler-dealers of the local underclass. As a journalist—and Hearn's writing about these characters is first-rate, if obsessively lurid—he was fascinated by their mores, their lingo and their songs. As such, Hearn came out of Cincinnati as a budding ethnographer, a man with a needle-sharp eye for the unseemly details of the street and the back alley. It is this gift and skill that he was later to apply to both New Orleans and his own special Japan, compiling, in the end, what becomes an oeuvre of ethnographic studies on everything from gumbo to geishas.

It is not an exaggeration to say that Hearn was run out of Cincinnati, nor is it one to add that he ran out on Alethea himself when he went south to New Orleans to leave it all behind him.

As for New Orleans, the city had prospered in the years leading up to mid-century, the Mississippi steamboats having transformed it into a major banking and trading metropolis. Tobacco, sugar and, especially, cotton were transported from plantations downriver to this port city, then on to markets around the world. But Hearn arrived there in 1877, twelve years after the South's defeat, which had brought with it the downfall of the one institution that had supported those three primary industries: slavery. The New Orleans that Hearn saw was a has-been town of mixed-blood people and colorful tales of the past, a perfect match for his own temperament and talents. The languorous atmosphere of New Orleans, then a shadow of its pre-Civil War self, appealed to a man who had now decided to spend his life looking for truth precisely there, in the shadows.

In America, he was drawn to detail and those topics ignored or neglected by mainstream writers. His letters and writings are full of anecdotes and ditties, words, songs, phrases and explanations of eerie customs intertwined with long-lost beliefs. This is where the pre-Japan Hearn and the Hearn that the Japanese so deeply admire merge, in his ability to record the features of a place's underbelly as if testifying to the locals' own lack of interest in it. Hearn is forever atop his own little steamboat, running upstream, as if seeking the source of things, while the masses are scrambling past him in whatever vehicles they can muster toward a future goal called "progress" that he would, till the day he died, refuse to see as anything but a false destination.

In New Orleans he studied the city's six Creole dialects and their many proverbs. Many articles from his New Orleans period may be about pat, if curious, customs, but sometimes he uncovers an intriguing story, like the one in "Saint Malo: A Lacustrine Village in Louisiana" that appeared in *Harper's Weekly* on March 31, 1883. This piece is about a settlement of Tagalas, or Philippine, fishermen. They were originally seamen who jumped their Spanish ship in Mexico, crossed over to the Gulf and came to live in Louisiana. Like much of Hearn's writing of the period, this is a rather undistinguished travel piece, but it does seem to constitute the first recording of a Filipino community in America. Hearn's instincts often led him to the right place. It was his unique outlook on the miseries of non-mainstream society—not his brilliant prose style—that made him a pioneering documentarist of ethnic America.

New Orleans in the 1880s had a huge transient population of sailors, migrants, and opportunity seekers. This made it a city with countless hotels, eating establishments of all sorts, gambling dens and brothels. In Cincinnati Hearn had published approximately 450 articles in five years. As in Cincinnati, he was prolific in New Orleans, writing not only his usual articles but also editorials, book reviews and drama critiques, as well as drawing hundreds of sketches. He published translations from French, in which he was extremely proficient, including, among others, the works of Guy de Maupassant, Pierre Loti and Emile Zola.

But even in his relatively early days in New Orleans, Hearn began to tire of the city. He wrote to his friend, musicologist Henry Edward Krehbiel, in February 1881, "I am very weary of New Orleans. The first delightful impression it produced has vanished. . . . What remains is something horrible like the tombs here—material and moral rottenness which no pen can do justice to."

He had certainly fallen on rough times in New Orleans—he was virtually on the edge of starvation there—and this set the stage for his departure to Japan. He briefly traveled north to see some old friends, whose meager hospitality failed to impress him, and then set out on his final and most sublime journey.

Hearn set foot on Japanese soil for the first time at Yokohama on April 4, 1890. It is fair to say that he felt at home from the beginning. Unlike virtually all other visitors to Japan from the West, he did not see himself as a preaching representative of a superior culture. He was in Japan to absorb its culture, not to sermonize his own. He threw himself into his new exotic garden with a genuine sense of wonder and discovery, setting out a patch for himself that other Westerners had little interest in, and then cultivating it with an intense passion.

He gravitated naturally, given his predilections, to the esoteric and mystical, introducing them as exemplary and representative. And as he observed, examined and wrote, he realized that he had finally found an identity for himself: Lafcadio Hearn—Chief Recorder of the Vanishing Japan.

As such, Hearn established a pattern of writing about Japan that lasted a century. A host of Western writers on the life of the Japanese continued in the Hearnian tradition, bewailing to their readers, and to any Japanese people who would listen, the tragic loss of all things good, quaint, mysterious, odd, macabre and "Japanese."

Thanks to the good offices of Prof. Basil Hall Chamberlain of Tokyo Imperial University (now the University of Tokyo), who was to help him get a position some six years later in Tokyo as well, Hearn landed a job teaching English at a middle school in the town of Matsue, arriving there for the autumn term that began in September 1890. Though he spent only about a year there as a teacher, he has been associated with this town on the Sea of Japan coast ever since. In a way this makes sense, for it was in Matsue that he first delved into those areas of religious prac-

The Life of Lafcadio Hearn

tice, provincial custom and folklore that were to form the vantage points of his outlook on Japan.

His view of Japan was set in its mold there, changing in the future only in the variety of its glazes. In Matsue he cast himself as a collector of miscellany, the same kind of transcriber of local mentalities that he had been in America. He was drawn to everything that the Japanese were tossing away, countless bits of information on cultural mores and religious ritual, from the gestures of Bon dances, Buddhist festivals, and pipe stems for males and females to the number of flickers made by an excited Japanese firefly. He was interested in ceremonial food, dress, poetry, music, the geisha, philosophy, flora and fauna, suicide, the Japanese smile, the Japanese tear, the Japanese sigh. Name a field of study of traditional art or life and Lafcadio Hearn was intrigued by it, swept away by it. He is the founding father of the school of Japanese uniqueness, the fountain that provides the spiritual and esthetic nourishment, flowing whenever turned on, that Japanese people required to convince themselves that they were more than the sum of their borrowed and mechanically transformed parts.

In Matsue, in February 1891, he married Setsu Koizumi, who was nearly eighteen years his junior, and the couple, together with members of her family and servants, moved to Kumamoto in Kyushu, where Hearn had accepted a teaching position at a high school.

Even in his early years in Japan, however, Hearn was beginning to tire of his elevated station and the responsibilities that went with it. Yet, it was already becoming too late to do much about it. The birth of a son, Kazuo, to whom Hearn, apparently at the expense of three children born subsequently, was profoundly devoted; his acquisition in 1896 of Japanese citizenship and a Japanese name, Yakumo Koizumi, through adoption by marriage; and the increasing burden of supporting his extended family—all these kept him in Japan. The main reason for his naturalization was his consideration for Setsu and Kazuo. Had he died a British subject in Japan, she could not have inherited his property.

By becoming a Japanese, however, Hearn further isolated himself from the foreign community in Japan, which saw itself, by virtue of birthright and skin color, as a culturally superior body surrounded by aimless copycat Orientals bent on the impossible, that is, becoming their equals.

It was in Kumamoto that he passed the most unhappy spell, labeling the town "the most horrible place in Japan." For one thing he had never been accustomed to looking after anyone but himself. Now he had a family, a burden he had dreaded since youth. He also began to see an ominous trend in his beloved adopted country. Japan had set itself on the path of empire, forcing its interests upon Asia. Hearn, an enemy of empire West and East, dearly wished for Japan to abandon the rush to the modern. In a speech delivered in Kumamoto on January 27, 1894, he said, "In the case of Japan, I think, there is a possible danger—the danger of abandoning the old, simple, healthy, natural, sober, honest way of living. I think Japan will be strong as long as she preserves her simplicity."

In other words, Hearn saw Japan following the trail blazed by the West, one that led to colonies and national aggrandizement, and he, who barely spoke or wrote Japanese but was now a self-styled expert on "the real Japan," was urging them to stay simple and ascetic. That was where Japan's beauty resided, he believed: in traditional simplicity and stoic austerity. And yet . . . he wanted the West to stand up and take notice of Japan. This is the contradiction of Lafcadio Hearn, one that came to be mirrored often in the twentieth century: The Westerner who supported a Japan brimming with accomplishment and pride but who cringed when its citizens began acting accomplished and prideful "like us."

In July 1894 Hearn abandoned teaching and returned to journalism, joining the staff of the *Kobe Chronicle* for a short time (October to December 1894) until his eyesight failed him. Kobe was a bustling port city, whose movers and shakers were intent on wholesale Westernization. Hearn, antipathetic to Western racist views of Orientals, increasingly saw himself as being on the Japanese side of things, so long as that side was traditional.

He was still idealizing his Japan. He wrote to Chamberlain at the time, "The Japanese peasant is ten times more of a gentleman than a foreign merchant could ever learn to be." But this idealization did not apply to Japanese officials or any Japanese, for that matter, who supported modernization of his country. These Hearn despised more than ever, as he did the foreign missionaries, who he believed had come to rob Japan of its true spirituality. (He wrote that the Christian faith "represents an undeveloped mental structure.")

Hearn recognized that he was out of step with the reality of his adopted land. "I felt as never before," he wrote to Chamberlain from Kobe, "how utterly dead Old Japan is and how ugly New Japan is becoming. I thought, how useless to write about things which have ceased to exist."

In August 1896 he made his final move in Japan, to Tokyo, taking up a teaching position at Tokyo Imperial University. He taught there until 1903, when a controversy erupted over whether he should have an inflated foreigner's salary or a normal Japanese one.

In Tokyo he was more than ever out of step with all those around him. In his eyes, the capital represented for Japan what New York ("this beastly machinery") represented for America. He craved peace of mind and subtle riddles, the charm of things that had vanished for most people but whose outlines and shadows he saw so clearly. Tokyo was confusion and the aping of the most rotten aspects of Western civilization, beauty replaced by a mechanics run mad.

The news of the eruption of Mount Pelée on Martinique in May 1902, killing thirty thousand people, stunned him. His health was deteriorating. A heart complaint that had dogged him for years, exacerbated by a near fatal bout of dengue fever in his New Orleans days, returned. In April 1904, he transferred to

Waseda University, but that was not to last long. On September 26, his heart gave out and he passed away.

Hearn's death in 1904 was greeted largely with indifference by the members of the foreign community who knew of him. The missionaries must have been much relieved. Hearn even managed to thumb his nose posthumously at them by choosing to be buried with a Buddhist ceremony. As for the Japanese, though many professors and students attended the funeral, as they would for a senior member of staff, little notice was taken of the event outside of his own academic circle. The Japanese had not yet recognized him as the adopted son of their forgotten past.

In America, however, he had built himself quite a reputation as an interpreter of Japanese life. The popularity of Japan after the country's victory in the war with Russia helped enhance Hearn's position as one of the few Westerners who understood the workings of the Japanese mind. But, as the century wore on, with the Japanese empire expanding in Asia, and Western empires becoming wary of it as a rival to their own imperial ambitions, it was not long before his reputation began to grow in Japan and wane in the West. In Japan Hearn was seen as a Western man of letters who sympathized with Japanese causes; in the West, as a second-rate and unoriginal apologist for Japanese nationalism. This is where the gap opened that has only widened since, though the notion of him as an apologist has vanished.

The Japanese took up Hearn, exalting him because he was unlike the other Europeans who had come to Japan at the time. His rejection of the values of his Christian education and his craftsman-like approach to and immersion in the subcultures of middle and southern America had prepared him well. He arrived in Japan immaculately prepared to absorb precisely those elegantly grotesque and moribund features of Japanese legend that the Japanese of the Meiji era had no time for themselves. As such, his writing could be usefully recycled by the Japanese as a record of their past when it became convenient for them, in the Taisho and early Showa eras (approximately 1912-1940), to conjure it up. You

The Life of Lafcadio Hearn

see, they could say, we are not only equal to you Europeans in our technological prowess, we also have a spiritual base that is profound, subtle and mysterious . . . and so different from your own.

As for the West, Hearn's legacy is that of an interpreter of all that is receding, an originator of the "tale of the vanishing Japan" that dominated Western views of this country for one hundred-odd years. Foreigners are drawn to this Japan, taking on the role of urging the Japanese to hold onto an elusive cultural identity that they have seemingly long abandoned. Yet if this model is true, and the "real" Japan has been vanishing for over a century, it is a miracle there is anything left of the country today at all.

This deep fissure in the two perceptions of Hearn and his legacy—a shining god on the one side and a minor transcriber of the weird and curious on the other—has obscured the real Lafcadio Hearn from view. The man, an authentic outsider to any time and place, a complex individual who rejected his own civilization and his own century's values, a faithful representative of nothing more or less than his own bizarre and wonderful imagination, stands somewhere in the shadows far below it all.

In the more than a century since the death of Lafcadio Hearn, the Japanese people have studiously formulated and maintained a myth; and they have done it with all the tools and vigor of nostalgia at their disposal. His collection of ghost stories titled *Kwaidan: Stories and Studies of Strange Things* is his work of the most enduring popularity in Japan, and this work alone has assured him a place in their hearts. No other foreigner, so this popular myth goes, has been as privy to Japanese secrets, or as devoted to their imaginative recreation; no foreigner then or since has loved Japan as deeply.

In the West, meanwhile, Hearn is a misunderstood mystery of a man who seemed to identify solely with cultural phenomena that had passed their sell-by dates. It was almost as if this man had to re-create a past before he could start living in the present.

As for the man himself, there is no doubt he had become disillusioned—the perfect word for Hearn—with his adopted country. Hearn had never had much time for the new Japanese male, whom he saw as an arrogant copyist of decadent Western ways, and he was thoroughly disgruntled with the treatment he was receiving in "the new Japan." His only choice was to go back to the country that made him into a writer in the first place—America—where, during his final months of life, he was planning a series of lectures and hoping to land an academic job.

In a letter to the British Japanologist Arthur Diosy, dated April 28, 1903, Hearn wrote, "Perhaps you do not know that most of my books were written under great disadvantage. I did the best I could, almost alone, and the result has been well-spoken of by European men of letters. But in Japan, all this has been studiously ignored."

Hearn was an outsider who had found, at last, his natural home in Japan. But he was too restless and melancholic, too trapped by personal obsessions, and too disaffected with his surroundings and his times to realize just how good his fortune was. His books on Japanese themes gained him a formidable reputation in the West. But as Japan pressed further and further in its imperial drive, Western readers began to view his preoccupations with the ideal, the exquisite and the spiritual as irrelevant.

Lafcadio Hearn was rootless and felt at home nowhere. Even after more than a decade in Japan, with a high salary and a large family that relied upon him in every way, with a growing stack of books to his name and personal deference paid him from the Japanese community (as any professor would receive), he wished to leave this country. Had he lived, he might have gone back to America. There was a potential job offer from Cornell University, which, in the end, did not pan out. He also toyed with the idea of moving to Manila, perhaps a thought that occurred to him because of the article he wrote about Filipinos who had found their way to the United States, or perhaps because it was warm there, and the warmth eased discomfort in his eye.

The Life of Lafcadio Hearn

He died in Tokyo, age fifty four. His father had died of malaria on his way back to Ireland from India, age forty eight. His mother had died, age fifty nine, in the National Mental Asylum at Corfu, the Greek island in the Ionian Sea.

But who was this intensely shy man of occult and, to the Victorian mindset, highly imprudent tastes, this freakish misfit who found solace for his imagination and, most important of all, respect for himself as a human being only in Japan?

It is to answer this question—and to address the further and more universal question of what it means to be a foreigner in any land, in any era—that I wrote *The Dream of Lafcadio Hearn*.

Tokyo
February 2011

The Dream of Lafcadio Hearn

Foreword

I am now finished writing all of this down, now that the shadows have come and gone, and can see with perfect clarity what my life entailed . . . who I, in fact, was . . . up to the very moment that I set a foot on Japanese soil.

It was that single gesture, the right foot extending, rising, hanging for an instant in the air then coming down, with the hesitation of the sea that lingered in it, onto a splintered wooden plank of the Yokohama dock. Before my left foot touched that wood my entire life of nearly forty years had flashed through my brain, with each and every event ordered as it had never been ordered before. That one step gave my life sense.

But it was not until some time later, when I first set my eye on the old coastal town of Matsue, that yet another life was set in motion, a life of another place and, dare I say, another time.

1890–1891   Matsue

When did I first enter into this last, and sublime, illusion? Perhaps it was the morning my mother abandoned me and Ireland to return to her native island in Greece. I never saw her again and, in fact, I kept only a single memory of her. I often said that I could picture her face, but this was a lie. I did picture a face but it was not that of my real mother. It was rather one of my own subsequent configurating. Later my father died at Suez and was buried at sea. His contours were finer in my mind . . . but I had made a point since childhood of relegating them to fantasy by merging them with those of a ghost I once saw wriggling on my bedroom door in the middle of the night. From the beginning I needed oceans to keep me separate from the ordinary reality.

The final image of my deep sleep of 1890 was that of an enormous river, black, and chunky as coal, with russet lights flickering on its bed. Boats sat unmoving on top of this pitch, upside-down. Drum-like sounds came from below. Was this the Mississippi or some other river that I had known? I could not place it and lay, bathed in sweat, for the moment trying to remember where this picture had originated. I gave up.

I moved the thin top quilt of my futon off my neck by wiggling my toes forward and back. As it inched down I wiped my neck of the sweat with the long sleeve of my *yukata*, a summer kimono. Why had I gone to bed wearing it? I closed my eyes and strained to recall what had happened the night before. Nothing came to me. I tried to put together the pieces of my voyage to Japan, to catch even a single detail, anything, of the long land journey to Matsue. A pitch-black hard rock body of water, with jagged static waves, was all I could see, and the drum-like noises coming from the overturned hulls all that I could hear.

I sat up. The room was a small one of four-and-a-half tatami mats, and by the head of my futon was a squat lamp made of rice paper and thick red lacquer. The candle inside it had burned out. I touched the lacquer frame. It was exceedingly cold, almost as cold as ice. Without standing I reached back far over my head to the sliding door that covered the window. It was dawn. I slid open the rice paper door that shaded the window. Outside it was light. Summer. The waves were breaking in the distance, between me and them a flat stretch of smooth pebbles and sand.

I left the room via the window, finding myself on that stretch between the inn and the sea. There were frogs hiding in a few bushes. I purposely wended my way, barefoot, far around them, so as not to disturb their singing. Grasshoppers jumped out of my way. One of them insisted on jumping straight ahead. I could not get rid of him. When one more jump would have sent him into the sea, I kneeled down to pick him up. But he must have hopped off while I was kneeling, for he was gone by the time I was there.

The tide was out and the waves were a mere ripple. I looked back at the inn. It was an old two-story structure of angled wood and rippled glass. Many such Japanese houses, of which I had seen photographs while in America, lacked glass in their windows and had only sliding paper doors on the inside and heavy-planked shutters on the outside. The glass of the inn's windows was imperfect in spots, distorting the reflection. Distortion was my standard, and this pleased me. I pried open my blind left eye with my elongated fingernail to get a better look, to expose the dead ball, dead since the age of sixteen. This changed nothing, least of all the distortion.

Matsue

As I walked back to the inn I noticed the heavy rocks on the roof, no doubt there for the purpose of holding it down in a storm. This seemed to me a curious choice in a country renowned for its earthquakes. In the Occident one died by either fire or ice. Here it was the wind or earth. The gods here were clearly enjoying a gamble.

When I returned to my room the bedding was gone. A cup of green tea and a small round cake wrapped in semi-transparent rice paper were waiting for me on the low table. The door slid open as I touched the teacup. A handsome young man stood by it.

"If you look at us Japanese in that way, Mr. Hearn," he said, "we will think you are a ghost."

I apologized and abruptly stood up. I did not know whether or not to offer my hand to him.

"You speak English," I said.

"Yes. I am a teacher at the school where you will teach too. How do you do?"

He stepped through the doorway, sliding the door shut behind him, put out his hand and told me his name: Akira Hosoi. I shook his hand.

"If everybody here speaks English like you, there will be no need for the likes of me."

"Soon you will speak Japanese like us, I am sure, Mr. Hearn."

I doubted that. He sat down at the table. The voice of a female came from the hallway. I did not understand what she was saying. The door slid open, and a young woman appeared carrying a cup of tea and a cake similar to mine on a tray. She entered, kneeled down, put the tray on the tatami mat, slid the door shut, then shuffled on her knees to the table and placed the tray on it, exchanging words with Akira.

"She says that she thought you had brought another man into the room last night."

"Another man?"

"Yes. She says that you spoke as if you were having an argument with someone in the middle of the night."

I explained that I often had arguments in my dreams and that it was normal. I solved all my philosophical problems while asleep and retained the waking hours for observation.

"I do not understand," he said.

The young woman spoke again.

"She says she hopes that no one at the inn caused an unpleasant experience for you."

"Quite the contrary," I said. "Now, where do we go from here?"

"Go from here?"

"Yes. What is the next move?"

"You must have breakfast."

"Not necessary. I'm ready to go with you, Akira. May I call you that?"

"Of course, Mr. Hearn. I am flattened by you."

"I think you mean 'flattered.'"

"Oh yes!" he said, laughing, as the young woman, covering her mouth, giggled for no apparent reason.

She spoke again, but Akira interrupted her gruffly. I asked what the matter could be.

"Never mind. She is so sorry."

"Sorry? Why?"

"Because she did not make chicken eggs for you for your breakfast."

"Chicken eggs? Who wants chicken eggs? I never eat anything for breakfast. What did she prepare?"

Akira asked her.

Matsue

"She prepared roots of lotuses and . . . and . . ."

He produced a small dictionary from his trouser pocket and leafed past some pages.

". . .and a small fish of the variety pleco-glos . . . plecoglossus altive . . . altive. . . ."

"Sounds delicious. Tell her I will have it."

"But we are due at your house shortly. The landlord waits for you."

"Landlords should be made to wait, Akira. It heightens their senses. Please tell the young lady to bring on the lotus roots and the . . . fish."

Akira said a few words to her in a harsh, commanding tone. The woman bowed, stood, walked to the door, kneeled at its threshold, slid it open, crawled out and closed it.

I asked if I had done the wrong thing.

"The wrong thing? You can never do the wrong thing here."

His outlines were already clear to me. Akira was a fine man, the best possible representative of his countrymen. He was modest yet straightforward, polite yet lacking in that fawning obsequiousness toward everything Occidental. This country was to have a miraculous future. I was now certain of it. In a mere century from now we would class the Japanese as we do the superior prosperous lasting cultures of our own tradition. This would be thanks to men like Akira Hosoi. The fawning gesture, the wheedling giggle, the feigned embarrassment, which I had already seen on my voyage, on my stay in Yokohama and the overland journey here to Matsue, were what was to be feared. It could turn into arrogance at the drop of a coin. Now I closed my eye and savored the trip in every detail. This excellent morning had brought it back to me.

I had decided to leave my revolver in America. Japan was a civilized country where Occidentals were respected. This at least was what Europeans and Americans had told me. They had felt secure in the integrity and the love of order of their Oriental hosts.

I understood that the Japanese were equally respectful of their animals, lest they offend the souls of those ancestors which had come to reside in their little bodies. This more than anything pleased me. The one time I nearly killed a man was due to his cruelty to an animal. I shot at him four times but, luckily for him, missed. He had picked up a cat that was winding its body, back hunched, about a pole. Holding its neck with his thumbs and middle fingers he proceeded to gouge out both its eyes with his index fingers. The cat managed wildly to scratch his wrists with its hind legs before he threw the miserable thing into the gutter and tromped on it with his boots. He went ahead strolling, whistling and sucking his wrists without so much as a backward glance. I witnessed the entire scene. I went to the cat. Had my eyesight been satisfactory a bullet would surely have struck the man in the back of his head. But the shots must have gone above it or astray to the side. I carried the blinded cat to a field, shot it through its mouth and buried it.

The young woman was impressed. I had finished every last morsel of my Japanese breakfast, though unable to maneuver the tiny crimson-lacquered pointed chopsticks with any degree of skill. Ever since the alms-taking days of my youth I had carried on my person a small spoon given to me by my pious great-aunt. I expected that I was the first Occidental ever to eat "Japanese sweetfish" (as my own, not well-worn, dictionary named it) with a Sheffield christening spoon. There is always some comfort in being the first to do anything.

"Does one eat the backbone as well?" I asked Akira.

He was standing with his back to me gazing at the sea. He did not immediately answer. Was he annoyed at me for disturbing his plans?

"Pardon me?" he said, turning about. "Oh, no. You should not eat it."

Matsue

There was an embarrassing pause. I looked toward the young woman.

"Well, how much do I owe?" I asked.

Once again there was silence.

"It has all been paid for. By the school. But you must give them a . . . a . . ." Akira reached once again for his ragged dictionary.

"Look, Akira, we cannot go on like this searching for every word. I will someday soon have to start learning Japanese. What is the Japanese word you want to say?"

"*Chadai*."

As Akira pronounced this word the woman lowered her head.

"*Cha-dai*."

"Yes. You understand!"

"No, I do not understand. I merely parroted your word. What does it mean?"

"It is, well, it is a gift of money to an innkeeper, to thank them for their kindnesses."

"I see. *Cha-dai*."

"Yes, you do understand."

I stood up and took two notes from the pocket of my trousers, which were draped over a large hinged rack in the corner. I approached the woman, who was still kneeling with bowed head, and held out the notes for her to take.

"Oh, you must not give it like that," said Akira. "I expected this, so I did bring what you must have now."

He took the notes from me and placed them on top of a sheet of rice paper in the palm of his hand. He carefully folded the paper around the notes, went to the woman, kneeled beside her and pushed the paper with the money inside it inch by inch toward her with stiffly outstretched fingers. The woman picked up the paper in both her hands and held it above her head for a moment. Once again she spoke.

"She says that you are a very kind man."

I blushed and, standing above her, bowed. I saw her for the last time some minutes later when I was putting on my shoes in the entryway. Beside me was the single battered valise which had seen me through years of travel from Ireland to County Durham, France to London, New York to Cincinnati, then throughout the South, the West Indies and finally to the most exotic location of all.

Why exotic? Were I to tell it once and for all I would put it down to the culture's insane propriety. Nowhere else that I had been did the people bind themselves with such rancor-producing obligatory regulations. I was determined to master these, for I believed, nonetheless prematurely, that they comprised the sole process through which the language itself could be mastered. If I were to be polite and enlightened, I would do so according to their instruction. This was no lone experiment on one man's part. It was a method of transforming oneself, at the age of forty, into another human being, one capable of inventing new ancestors for himself in order to be reborn in the most ideal guise imaginable.

Akira came from the outside into the entryway to find me on my hands and knees on the dirt floor. I was merely copying my hosts, the young woman, her husband and five-year-old son, all of whom were prostrate on the raised wooden floor on my behalf.

"You do so much more than you must, Mr. Hearn," he said. "You do not have to give so much money to them. You do not have to bow to them like that. You do not kneel on the soil."

He nevertheless smiled at me and took my valise. I sat in the rickshaw and, brushing the dust off the knees of my trousers, looked once again at the innkeeper and his family. They were still bowing in the same place and position. The little boy lifted his head to look at the bizarre spoon-wielding unshaven squatty Cyclops, but his mother, without so much as raising her own head,

Matsue

pushed him down by the nape of his neck. Akira, having fastened my valise to the back of the rickshaw, sat beside me and shouted at the rickshaw runner. The rickshaw jerked to a start, turned a half circle and started off. I closed my eye in order to hear the waves breaking on the other side of the inn. I was able to hear them perfectly. They were breaking in rhythm, a correct rhythm, an even hush that no one—neither one there to witness it himself nor one far away who must be told about it through the words of others—could possibly fault.

How on earth did I end up standing in front of a group of young boys in this Japanese country town, burdened with the duty of imparting knowledge to them? The very predicament alone amused me and gave rise to many more eerie and peculiar thoughts than my situation would warrant. Japan as a destination was, for me, no more incongruous a fate, if a slightly more unpredictable one, than anywhere else on the globe was or could have been. I had, after all, spent my years at my school in England as a roving and incorrigible prankster, the perfect role for a boy who could not fit in, whose "background" was, mildly considered with a polite clearing of the throat, "mixed." When accused of not being like all the rest and bullied, I replied with clowning, the standard ruse of the withdrawn.

Later, when I roamed the more pleasantly seedy regions of the American Midwest and South, I found a mixture of race to be the rule, one ignored by the "purer" elements of society but one destined to replace it, I sensed, with the force of its blood. Darkness of skin was my mark as a child and my lure as an adult. I was always tempted to consider it my true color and appreciated such skin in others, particularly women. I gave into the temptation and forfeited my independence only once, however, when I married an octoroon and learned—no, was taught—a lesson, that my inclination was a personal weakness and that my century was not the proper one for adventure in the flow of instinct.

Roger Pulvers

By what right was I there, in that classroom? No one in the world had ever taught me a thing, certainly not my father, his faith-stuttering relatives or the raw priests foisted upon me, innocent and bewildered. My father was more concerned with his other children than with me, with his dearly sought-after and safely bred second wife than with his first, whom he merely stumbled over while inspecting ruins. I was the product of that stumbling, a fitting metaphor for a boy who felt only ill and encased in the presence of religious conviction. I saw adults as human beings who stuffed faith into the orifices of children in the name of sustenance. Anything I was told, I distanced from knowledge; anything I was fed, I found covered in bloodletting fungus and slow-growing molds that eventually formed and grew of their own accord in the crevices of the brain. Now was I to be that agent of festering decay in the brains of others?

Those others were the ruddy-faced little boys in this village of battered charm, a cloud of their expressions now before my eyes, a landscape entreating me to be comprehensible, to give them something, anything, if but an atom of meaning that they could swat among themselves, stun, capture and, eventually, possess.

They were miraculously clean, as if scrubbing itself were the be-all of native morality. I had noticed this already about the Japanese even before coming to this remote district of the country. Poverty did not make them dirty. It was as if they doused their skin in order to show their neighbors that starvation, ignorance and cramping need not dent their souls. The exterior was where their entire individuality was seen to reside. Below this cloud of shocked faces was a sea of uniform blue, washed with charcoal specks—or so the cloth of their fatigued kimonos appeared in my eye, that place where the cloud and the fly-like atoms of something called "meaning" came together.

At first I had stood, waiting, outside the open classroom door. The boys were talking among themselves. Of course I could not follow their conversation. My entire Japanese vocabulary at the time consisted of *jinrikisha*, the English "rickshaw," *sayonara*,

Matsue

which I was told meant "If it must be thus," and *chadai*, which I took to mean a gratuity that one is obliged to pay to assuage the guilt incurred when someone has fulfilled an obligation of kindness toward one . . . or something to that effect. As for the rest, I was getting by on my smooth bow and my perpetually embarrassed stance. Being squatty, intensely shy and myopic helped.

No sooner had I stepped through the door than did the terror-stricken boys turn in their places, stiffen and sit. One of them shouted a word, which I was soon to add to my vocabulary, the equivalent of "Rise!" They rose instantly. The same boy exclaimed again, and the mass folded its neck, blackening my lovely cloud. This over with, they sat in their seats and stared straight ahead. I took off my wide-brim hat, that companion of mine under which, half-hidden, I had always felt invulnerable to ghosts snapping foully at me from people's mouths, and flung it toward the table that stood on a small platform at the front of the room. The hat missed its mark, landing half off the platform and half on. I pointed to it and smiled. The boys continued to look straight ahead with faces that some might describe as "expressionless." This fixation of the eyes was their protection against the incomprehensible. It was certainly not expressionless. It was merely *response-less*. I felt an intense envy for this trait and, more than anything, desired to possess it. In the past it would have saved me the greater part of my adolescent and adult anguish, an anguish which infected me from dark skin to spirit. I had no armor, only a skeleton, and that too creaked with a self-punishing dread. And to think I could have been saved all these years by a single expression that passed for the lack of one!

I walked up to my hat, picked it up and, ceremoniously, placed it on the table. Should I point to it and say "hat"? "The hat is on the table"? "The hat was not on the table"? "The teacher—or the man who is propped up before you like a balloon on a twisted thread—is supremely desirous of your knowing that one can live on twenty cents a day for the worse part of one's life then be thrust elsewhere, namely here, and be treated with respect thanks to one's birthright." Why my birthright and not yours? Why are you not looming over me—considering my stature it would not be difficult—and teaching me your little sounds for "wide brim" and "empty balloon" and "response-less respect"? Had I a soul it might find position in your own seed. I might enter that cycle at any minute, thereby losing my self in the most peculiar yet natural way. I could become you, you know. I could.

But there was nothing at all that I could tell them at that moment, nothing to bring the cloud closer to my own face or untwist the thread or tear it with the most monstrous strangling grip. I walked among them, down each aisle, occasionally placing a finger on a desk, occasionally stopping for the sake of stopping. This all evoked not so much as a sidelong wink. As I walked I told them, in long slow tones, about my accidental birth, my upbringing, my scavenging in the rubbish pits of London and my passage to America. I left nothing out in the fifty-minute monologue, save for my forays into the brothels and my sniffing over corpses in the morgues, hideous eyesight and coin-size nostrils being the true friends of a morbid curiosity. Distance and time added nothing to perspective. I had realized from a young age that perspective only made insensible things *appear* rational. Order is not truth.

I knew from my very first days in Yokohama and its rural environs that I should adore Japan, for it was a land totally lacking in perspective, a land of extreme and jumbled passions which nevertheless displayed a single unmoved and seemingly indifferent gaze. These boys had nothing to learn from me. I had everything to learn from them. My task was to motivate them to give me what I had to have: a calcic resolve, a word, phrase, expression or style which I could begin to fashion and manufacture by myself, a substance which I could inject into my skin and allow to seep into my marrow. Without it I would die here, I knew, from a softness of bone, just as I had died everywhere I had been before. My skeleton would collapse of its own meager weight.

In the final fifteen seconds of the hour, after a prolonged and terrifying silence, I put my face directly in front of that of one

Matsue

of the boys. He stared at me as before, not so much as blinking, not emitting a breath of terror on the glue-hardened slit of my eye. To all appearances he was holding his breath. I opened my mouth. That was the clincher. He must have been momentarily overpowered by the sheer stench coming out of it. He seemed to gag, but nonetheless bravely maintained the clamp on his lips. I took my pipe, its bowl still full of ash, from my trouser pocket and held it between my face and his. Should I say, "This is a pipe, this is my pipe, the pipe of the most famous police reporter in all Cincinnati, of the most notorious dissecting-room rat in all Louisiana, of the most wretched man ever to set foot on the soil of this country, suddenly expected to be, of all things, a teacher! Yes, of all the goddamned hellish and perverse things in this world, a . . ."? Should I turn this visual standoff into a lesson and redeem my status? Yes, this little boy, doubtless the son of an ignorant, illiterate and superstitious mother and father, the poorest peasants in this poor land, this vessel of brash indifference, this empty card sitting on its edge, upright, in its pack, would, in the remaining ten seconds of our shared hour, be able to hear for the first time in his life, in a language which he could not distinguish from the lolling tongues of African primitives, words flowing out of my stinking mouth that might, just might, make perfect sense to him. He would understand in two seconds the esoterica of Maltese influences on the architecture of the southern Ionian islands, of the bastard abandonment of anomalous and unwanted issue, of the similarity of one's chapped hands when one is begging for food on a street and when one is feeling the skin surrounding the genitals of the opposite sex, of the necessary ingredients in a true Creole *gombo* (oh yes, it *must* contain a preparation of dried and pounded sassafras leaves!) and, most important of all, in the entire world, by God, of the absolutely proper lilting tone in the Irish voice of women who have taught one "everything you need to know" when they sing, exclusively on one's humble, if diminutive, behalf, "Believe Me If All Those Endearing Young Charms." The boy would understand all of this, I knew, merely from staring down into the large black hole in my face, and I would still have three seconds left to allow him to breathe.

I was a gifted teacher, I realized that then. Who else could have imparted such exotic knowledge merely through foul scents, globe-like looks and unpracticed gestures? I knew that I could have been, in a former era, a diplomat, a politician, perhaps a wise leader in ancient Greece or Rome or America—who knows, even an introspective juba-slapping darky-malarky Rutherford B. Hayes!

I wanted to tell my boy that in the final second of our lesson. But enough was enough. A teacher can make the error of overburdening his wards with details of little rhyme and less reason. Better to leave some things unsaid. On that thought, the hour ticked to an end. I stood up straight and closed my mouth, and with my pipe sticking out of it, walked backwards, methodically, toward the front of the room. I reached behind my back, groped for my hat and picked it up. I lowered the brim over my head until its edge touched the bowl of my pipe. I could not see my boys now, but I could hear them. The same boy from before made his exclamation. They all rose. At his further command they bowed, or so I heard. I stumbled toward the door as if in a totally darkened space. I easily found the knob, turned it, opened the door and made my exit. I left them standing, heads bowed, a mass of intense black telling me, that first day, all I needed to know.

I had felt a sense of deep accomplishment from my first hour. By studying me my pupils would gain knowledge of the outside world—the world outside Matsue, that is—and of Occidentals, the way we were. I was to be their model. So I resolved to tell them in the second encounter about the honor bestowed upon me when I was asked by my dearest friend in Cincinnati to be his second in a duel. Dr. Partridge's only weakness was a monumental conceit. He was so sure of himself that he condescended to select me as his

Matsue

second. This, I knew, would amuse these boys with their inherited tradition of reckless revenge.

I was chuckling as I walked, diagonally, across the grounds of the castle, now in ruins. An enormous twisted pine tree, its fat gnarled branch upheld by a T-shaped crutch, grew out of the moat's embankment. I passed under it and sat on a large flat stone embedded in the soil. I stacked the eight books I had brought with me on my lap. I must have dozed off, for the next thing I knew I was prostrate on the ground, the books spilling over themselves down the embankment. Spencer was in the mud; Baudelaire, in the water. I amused myself with the thought of the philosopher's Great Doubt being soiled and of the poet's malodorous flowers taking root, the former producing a pinkish brain of enormous proportions, and the latter giving rise to a stunning lotus blossom in the shape of pudenda, opening up a fiery red, two impressive Occidental organs, new objects of worship for these superstitious, hungry natives.

At that moment I heard the sounds of singing coming from the other side of the castle wall. I could not make out the song, however. The voices were both male and female. I could not even make out the language they were singing in. It did not seem to be Japanese to me.

I left my scattered books where they were and hopped onto a rock in the middle of the shallow moat. A second giant's stride brought me flush against the wall. I put my cheek to it. The chisel marks were still visible along the pointed edges of its massive blocks. Leaving my shoes at the bottom of the wall I put my feet carefully into the crevices between the blocks and began to climb. Luckily the wall had been built on a slight angle rather than straight up and down. With a firm grip on each block I managed to make my way to the very top. I lifted my chin over the top and peered down on the clearing below. There were two groups of school children, somewhat older than my wards, standing at some distance from each other. One group, the boys, was dressed in watercolor blue. The other, the girls, was in kimonos of many colors. They looked like compact rows of mechanical dolls.

It was still hard for me to distinguish the songs and the words. This must have been some sort of choir practice, for the two groups were led by separate instructors, both male, who were moving their arms in gentle, waving gestures. I closed my eye and focused on the sounds. Immediately they separated. The boys were singing a spirited song in Japanese. The girls were singing in English, or what certainly—well, perhaps not certainly—resembled English. The song was "Auld Lang Syne." I opened my eye to take in the little toy scene, then looked back at the propped-up pine. It was then that I noticed a snake not more than a foot from my face. I adjusted my grip on the blocks and turned fully toward it. I raised an eyebrow and inhaled deeply.

"I know you," I said to it.

The snake turned its head and, body following, glided back along the top of the wall and, somewhere in the blur, down it. I sniggered in delight as the two choir groups came to the climaxes of their songs. It must have been the sniggering that caused me to lose my balance. But I did not fall. I merely slid down the wall at a somewhat faster rate than I had ascended it, landing squarely on top of my shoes. Once down I saw that I had torn the fly off my trousers. All three of its buttons had been sheared off. I bent down to look for them. But a man such as one whom only the most expert or profoundly conceited of marksmen would choose as his second could hardly hope to find such minute objects. I soothed my pique with the thought that my fly buttons were probably at the bottom of the moat, in the mud mingling with Baudelaire's wicked seed.

I walked back, diagonally, across the castle yard, holding my eight books, wettest one on top, in my right hand and my wide-brim hat over my crotch in my left. Turning the corner where the castle wall fell off into neglected rubble, I crossed paths with the two groups of pupils. All of them, boys and girls and instructors

Matsue

alike, bowed to me. They did not stop bowing until I was well past them. I put my hat on my head and held four books in each hand, as a Barnum & Bailey strongman does his dumbbells. These were my strength, not so much their content as their grandiose form and the miraculous way in which I—conceived on the soil of the same continent as the men who created them—cradled them, gripped them, displayed them and brandished them high in the air.

Were those two groups, now one united as if never separable again, watching me as I strode away from them, or were they still bowing their heads, afraid to see me as I am until passing out of their sight? Were they bowing to a teacher, a man of learning and exotic experience, or to an individual, that is, to me, Patricio Lafcadio Tessima Carlos Hearn, the only Occidental who could readily be recognized by a Japanese snake on an angled wall so far from what everyone else in this world like him calls home?

I was ideally suited to this country in every way except one. What good was my spectacular sense of smell in a place so thoroughly lacking in scents? For some days I had actually entertained the idea that my unique gift had become dulled. Then it occurred to me that the Japanese possessed such insignificant nostrils because, due to the evolution of their culture, no need arose to enlarge them. Aesthetic Darwinism. But how I longed for the parsnip fritters, the nougat fruitcake, the marrowfat peas and the hairy okra taken to America by the slave trade, my pungent adopted cuisine prepared by my cacao women, buxom ex-slaves. It inspired me. I still damned myself for having fallen in love with the Negress in Cincinnati. I took her on. I took on her child by another man. I lost my friends and my career there over this. Only when three years had beaten sense into my Greek-Irish skull—not a happy combination when you consider the protrusions and hollows it would create once the flesh and organs had sloughed off it—was I able to rid myself of that well-built country girl, the first woman to witness the furtive motions of a man who, as yet, cast no shadows.

Now, more than a decade later, she came back to me rarely. But it was as if her scent, having accompanied me, remained with me despite the fog of pipe smoke that normally enveloped my head. That scent mingled with the recalled fragrance of the peas and okra, spoiling nostalgia forever. I would have to find a new nostalgia here.

I was smoking a pipe. My cat, Edgar, was perched atop my valise, which, when laid on my lap, doubled as a desk. Just beside Edgar's nose on the shelf was a book on Japanese insects. The confusing spring was over. The summer vacation had given me a chance to read and meditate. I had resigned myself to my symbolic role: fearless educator of Japan's young. Secretly they were educating me. I had begun to write about the country. I had begun to replace my sense of smell with a new sense, a cross between vision and touch, a sense that would allow me to surrender myself willingly to the exquisite, to lose myself to the delicate, and to abandon the brash and domineering quality that was my inheritance. My Japan would be nurtured entirely within the pales of this crossed sense.

A mosquito was circling Edgar's unperturbed head. This was the Edgar who did not so much as wince at the acrid billows of smoke accumulating around him. I had named him after Poe. After all, I used to be called "the raven" myself. My cat would be my creator. I stroked his head, and the mosquito landed on the back of my hand. With my other hand I smacked it gently, once. I carefully lifted my palm and examined the mosquito with my magnifying glass. I was pleased to see that I had been successful in my attempt to kill it without doing much damage to its body. In fact, it was just dying under my gaze through the glass. Its crushed legs shook rapidly from side to side then stopped, with the tiniest droplet of blood—my own—covering its head, a soft reddish amber that would, I imagined, preserve this part of its body forever, just as is. I told Edgar to go and sit on the verandah.

Matsue

Without requiring a gesture he followed my order. I placed the mosquito on the surface of my magnifying glass and opened the book to the section on them. I meticulously compared my mosquito with those in the book. I lowered my eye to the text, studying its fine-line drawings. I located what I thought was a similar one to mine, then tipped the glass over. My mosquito landed beside its two-dimensional sister. I snapped the book closed. I felt an intense rush of pleasure: Lafcadio Hearn's blood mixed with that of the Japanese mosquito *Culex tritaeniorhynchus*. Some might have thought this a "perverse pleasure." But to me it was the most natural pleasure in the world. Hence, it followed that I was an imperfect and singularly unqualified man to teach these people enlightenment and civilization.

The front door downstairs slid open, and a voice came to me in English.

"Mr. Hearn?"

"Come up, Akira," I called to him. "No, on second thought, stay there."

I told Edgar that I was going downstairs and left my pipe on my valise desk beside my magnifying glass and the copy of *Japanese Insects* by Dr. H. Tanaka, Ph.D. Edgar appeared to be either indifferent or asleep.

Akira and I sat in the garden of my house, he on a small low rock and I on a large one.

"Do not get the idea that I am placing you at my feet, heaven forbid," I told him.

"I do not understand, Mr. Hearn."

"Oh, what I want to say to you is, I want to be, for now, at your feet, at the feet of all Japanese. I must start over again in my learning. I must first become an empty slate if I am going to develop the sense I require to write about Japan."

"I am not sure that I understand what you say. But we want to learn so much from you. You are our teacher. You know about Europe and America, about how people can get culture and become *cilivized*. We Japanese are all very primitive people."

"Oh, Akira, it is not that way at all."

I stared at him with a squinted eye. He looked away.

Edgar was now sitting on the narrow ground-floor verandah. The garden and its two unequally placed humans must have been quite a sight in his eyes. Cats let on nothing. I admired that in them and the Japanese.

"I love the way the planks of the verandah fade from the outside edge in, as a matter of course," I said.

"We call that verandah a *nure-en*, a wet verandah. It is supposed to get the rain on it and slowly grow old like that."

"You see, Akira? It is a culture of genius to create something like that."

"No, professor, it is no culture. People are only poor. They do not have a roof. It is primitive. No culture. In Europe people build things forever. It is strong like stone and powerful culture."

"Listen, Akira, please listen. What is Europe? Things are built of marble and stone, it is true, but we Europeans then live in the shadow of that permanency. We can never get into the sun; we are forced to worship it with our necks craned upwards for century after century, kept in the dark. It is much better to recognize decay as the normal state of things, to let things rot and crumble. This is closer to truth."

Akira put his head in his hands and chuckled.

"Do you find this funny?" I asked.

"Funny? No. Your English is much too difficult for me. But even more difficult than that, professor, is what you think. We so much admire Europeans because they have what we need to have. Please do not teach us to remain as we are. We are not happy as

Matsue

we are. We are . . . we are . . . bad. Oh, I am sorry, I wish I could speak Japanese with you."

We sat in silence for some moments as it became quite dark. It was as wet as the nights on Martinique. Suddenly, in the space between me and Edgar, a firefly glowed, flitting about. I was not surprised to see one there, as I had read about them in *Japanese Insects* by Dr. H. Tanaka, Ph.D. Several more fireflies appeared, flickering in circles.

"They are apparently not like the fireflies of the Louisiana swamps," I told him. "Yours flicker twenty six times every second, but then increase this to sixty three times when gripped by fear."

Akira looked up at me. I felt ecstatic. I could teach these people something about themselves, something which originated with them but only took on significance when filtered through my newly acquired double sense. We were now surrounded by dozens upon dozens of flickering fireflies, a luminous crown for our heads.

"In winter we study by the light of reflected snow. In summer our light comes from fireflies kept in a bottle," he said. "These are our lamps for students to read books with. So we call our student days, let me see, our 'firefly-snow period.' You see?"

"There is poetry in your language unlike in any other I know."

"But no, professor, it is not poetry. It is just a phrase, very ordinary. Please understand. Please do not find so much good here when all is, as you say, rotting."

"Look, Akira, what are we struggling for? I now ask you to understand this. To make the lives of people in the future more comfortable? If so, why? Do we know them? Can we love them? Is it possible to see them? Look at me. Look at me, for Christ's sake! What do you see, eh? You think you see a person, but all you see is a single flashing illuminated outline. That is all. That is absolutely all, Akira!"

Edgar, jarred by my raised voice, bolted off his "wet verandah" into the house.

"You see? I even frighten my own cat."

"No, it was not you. You do not frighten anybody, professor. It was that."

Akira pointed to the narrow pebbled path at the foot of the verandah. A frog sat on it with his belly glowing from the inside.

"He swallow too many fireflies," said Akira.

I jumped off my rock, unable to contain my laughter. I found myself leaping up and down, first beside the rock, then by the frog, which remained in place all the while. Akira, like the frog, stayed where he was, smiling along with me. I knew that our minds were one at that moment and that the distinction of teacher and taught was no longer clear between us. I would have, on this night, to find a Japanese poem about fireflies. I would have to translate it, even without knowing the language. The language would be no barrier to me. The poem would be my poem until it transformed itself, becoming, once again, Japanese, the blood between us.

I was becoming more and more convinced that there was a mission here to accomplish, not one in God's name but one in ephemera's. How could the Japanese be made to see that their fever for things Occidental was the true sickness? How could they be led into a robust cynicism, away from their feverish quest for, as Akira so earnestly mispronounced it, cilivization? We were the ones whose minds were constricted.

I was glad that I had encountered Japan now, before our entire Occidental being was brought down, smothered and trampled by the lovely looking smooth monuments of our own fashioning. The Occident was "progressing" and would continue to "progress" for decades, but eventually, if I had my wish, it would be properly toppled by Japan, a Japan of doubting, a hollow-interior Japan, a

Matsue

Japan where the power of a single cicada's call could permeate the microscopic caverns in the monument's rock and smash it to dust.

This occurred to me on my daily late-summer walk through the streets of the town of Matsue. The stifling heat did not bother me. I was used to it from my months on Martinique. In the tropics my talent languished, my body surrendered its defenses, my mind shed its good sharp spikes. I was content to be feeble, for philosophy had done the human race not a whit of good at any time. Dismissing it had been bliss.

The six weeks of high fever which had overtaken me on Martinique alternated in my mind with the sights of my Matsue walk. I quickened my gait, as if to prove to myself that I had not been struck down at that moment. I adjusted my hat, that necessary parasol on my head, my shady friend. It allowed me to see the world without being seen myself, the all-observing eye, the writer's ideal instrument. I felt geography's miracle then, that I had finally been positioned on the precise dot where a tiny sphere— I— could roll along forever, encountering no friction.

I pictured myself climbing seven miles up Martinique's Mt. Pelée, swimming in the lake until exhausted—I was an excellent and powerful swimmer—until the cold penetrated my fat and invaded my organs. When I came to in Matsue, the memory had broken. The balm of daydreams had served me, as daydreams should. The eyesight in my single good eye gradually returned, though with each recurrence of recollection, I knew that I would be drained more and more of the sphere's fluid. Now, right now, I could see again. I would have to blot out the past if I was to continue to see.

The ordinary Matsue townspeople were turning away from me. They would rather not look at an unusual creature of such murky skin in their midst. I delicately tipped the brim of my hat, bowing to an elderly woman with blackened teeth. She stepped back so swiftly that she toppled into a shallow ditch. I offered her my hand like a gentleman, not removing my hat, for such a gruesomely lit face would have only startled her all the more. This gesture was as unfamiliar to her as was the tipping of the hat. The poor woman could only cover her face to rid herself of the presence of this now pale, if outwardly generous, ghost.

I walked on, looking back to see her scurry off, lifting the hem of her kimono. I vowed to have as much respect for people's sense of native propriety as I had disdain for their Occidentalized ideas. I had brought many faults of character with me and was now determined to rid myself of them, if only to please people here and abide by the unwritten regulations of Japanese decorum. But, as for my penchant for the grotesque deviations of observation and documentation, this was non-negotiable. I could no more deny that than shed the skin I was born with.

I was prepared to compromise virtually anything, even my convictions, if it would help me enter, together with the cicada's voice, into the Japanese rock. Once inside I would be part of a whole. Then the Japanese would accept me as an eternal witness. I was completely open to change for the first time in my life. Oh, I had always been receptive. Others may have seen me as recalcitrant, but that was their problem. They had been unable to see that I was enveloping them whole, each and every one of them. I went away a changed man. They remained themselves.

I was walking toward the temple gate to meet Akira, my brow dripping with perspiration that flowed over my eyebrow and into my eye. I was not going to wipe it away. I bathed my eye, and its constant companion, blur, cleared in ripples. I certainly would not permanently remove this hat, under no circumstances whatsoever. The only time I did remove it was in Philadelphia. I was forced to exchange it, temporarily, at a pawn broker's, for a less conspicuous covering, to please the all-compliant good, good people of that good, good town. I had received a letter while there, only months before coming to Japan, from a man purporting to be my brother. I asked him to prove it by post, which he did by sending me a photograph of our father. This was the very same father, mind you, who had lived in the West Indies some thirty years before

Matsue

I arrived there, the very same father who had married—or, not exactly married— a dark-skinned illiterate woman, some twenty five years before I had. Those facts alone nearly prompted me to turn back to a gray, hateful New York City and bury myself there. My brother had, like me, lived in Ohio and had read my articles published in Cincinnati. Why should I be forced to meet him? He wrote that we shared blood. Blood? Whose blood? Blood, which may have once been the same, changes drop by drop in its winding flow until, at some distance, there occurs a separation. Such blood would clash if compressed together. It must be avoided. No one now shared my blood. Absolutely no one!

I stopped under a large tree by a paddy field. The farmers were working among their rice plants, examining their ears. The tree resounded with a veritable string section of cicadas. I approached the trunk and looked up it. I started to shinny up the trunk, but the cicadas still did not stop their trilling. I was some six feet off the ground, with my head entirely inside the tree. I could see hundreds of them, a black mass. Resting my knee in the fork formed by two branches I removed my hat—it was even hotter in the tree than outside it—and waved it above my head, screaming to the players at the top of my lungs about the ominous steam rising out of Mt. Pelée, the mild tortures inflicted upon me at the crude hands of lewd boys, the filth of Covent Garden where I begged and, finally, the pickpockets and whores who plied their respective trades at Cincinnati society funerals. This not only satisfied me enormously, but it also shut up the cicadas. When I slid down the trunk and covered my head again, however, they resumed their music. The farmers, crouched in their paddies, stared at me with bulging faces, as if I were a Basque ghost. I doffed my hat to them, and a cicada flew out of it. They laughed raucously at this, and so did I. We had, indeed, found common ground in unsuspected juxtaposition. Who could now say that I was not, finally, on my own home ground?

Akira appeared peeved when I came close enough to see him standing by the temple gate.

"Professor, professor," he said.

"Good day, Akira. Hot, very hot."

"You come very late. I am waiting an hour here."

"I am sorry," I said. "You must realize that I have things to discover here. I have been in Japan but half a year. Would you chastise a babe of six months for natural sins?"

"Please, please learn Japanese quickly, Mr. Hearn. Then I will understand you."

"I am trying, Akira. Listen."

I told him what I thought to be the word for "metaphysics" in Japanese.

"Kay-gee-joh-gah-koo. Do you understand, eh?"

"I see," he said. "Yes."

"You understand, then?"

"I understand that I will probably not understand you any more if you speak Japanese than if you speak English."

I took him by the arm and we entered the temple grounds.

"Do you know what I did today on my way here, Akira?" I asked him, embracing him tightly.

"No," he said, squirming out of my grip.

"I conducted my first Japanese orchestra."

The temple grounds were a swarm of people, many of them, particularly the children, dressed in a colorful array of stripes and checks. I had never seen such a large number of small stalls, each one selling different trinkets, wooden or papier-mâché toys, masks, baubles and combs made of tortoiseshell or decorated lac-

Matsue

quer with inlaid mother-of-pearl, old prints and books, pottery of every shape, size and function. Some little boys were trying to trap goldfish from a large tub into fine handmade nets. One boy, having secured his catch, sprinted by me holding it in a glass filled with water. He was covering the top of it with his palm. As he ran by me his elbow brushed against my thigh, and the glass fell to the ground, his fat little goldfish, now out of the water, wriggling and writhing. I bent down beside the boy and smiled at him. But, taking one look at me at such close quarters, he sprang up and bolted toward the temple gate.

"Leave it. It's only a fish," said Akira.

"I thought you Japanese revered the souls of fish and animals. Who knows but that this single fish might be a repository for one's ancestor's soul?"

"Mr. Hearn, you should be teaching in this temple, I think, not in a modern school. My father is dead, but you say many similar things as he did."

We walked past a row of stalls selling woodblock prints and sundry pictures.

"These are so useless to us now," said Akira. "Only people from the country buy them."

"And foreigners," I said, examining a foot-high pile of colorful pictures.

"What's this one?" I asked.

"These are all Otsu-e, uh, pictures from the town of Otsu, near Kyoto. They are not printed. They are painted. They were once very popular, but now not so. People traveling from Tokyo to Kyoto used to stop off and buy them as cheap souvenirs. But two years ago the railway came there and now no one stops. So they die."

"What a shame. They are lovely."

"Lovely? I do not think so. They are so, how you say, primitive, rough. Only very simple people liked them. The artists never signed their names."

"I like this one. Why does he have such full sideburns going up from his cheeks?"

"This is Shoki. He fights disease. He is very powerful. I think he comes first from China."

"I want this one. Would you ask him how much it is?"

Akira asked the man at the stall the price of the painting. The man held up both hands with fingers spread. I reached into my pocket, brought out some money and handed him ten sen. The man exchanged an embarrassed glance with Akira, who swiftly covered my hand in his.

"The price is not ten sen but ten rin. Please do not pay him too much. It is not good for all of us if you do."

"Very well," I said. "Are these all Otsu paintings?"

"Yes, I think so."

"Very well."

I counted out a hundred of them, virtually the entire pile, and asked Akira, who stood by dumbfounded, to tell the man to wrap them in rice paper.

"Tell him that I'll pick them up on our way out."

Beside a large wooden bell tower were a number of tents with barkers in front of them luring reluctant festivalgoers with a loud and fast patter. I could not understand a word of it, of course, but it reminded me keenly of what I had witnessed in New Orleans. Wherever I went I felt that people of a particular trade or profession were much more akin in temperament and character to those who plied the same trade or practice, pursued the same profession, in another distant country than they were to their own countrymen who followed dissimilar callings. A Japanese barker looked to me like a Louisiana barker, blended into him, melded features

Matsue

with him, spoke his words at his pace and to the same shady effect. A sailor out of Liverpool was cut from the same rough cloth as one from Saint-Pierre. Nothing, not even the fiendish uniqueness of the Japanese manner, would convince me otherwise.

We were standing in front of a tent that featured a crudely painted giant rat.

"What's in there? I want to go in," I told Akira.

"This is not nice," he said. "You should not waste so much money."

"I won't give him too much this time. What's in there, tell me."

"He is saying that this is a very, very big mouse, as big as a 10-year-old child. He says as big as sheep."

"Hmmm, I'd like to see that. Most mice are too small for me to see. I think this one is just my size."

I handed the barker a coin and entered the dark tent. When I came out my eye ached from the strong light, and I walked right past Akira. He caught up with me.

"A kangaroo, Akira. A wallaby, to be more precise."

"*Warabi*? That is a so-called mountain vegetable. We eat it. Not an animal."

"Not *warabi*, Akira. Wall-a-by. From Australia. Never seen one before myself in the flesh, only in books. It was not a giant rat, but I am most satisfied by the deception."

Two drunken men, arm in arm, were describing shaky figure eights some twenty feet in front of us. They stopped simultaneously in their tracks and, necks bobbing, stared at me.

"Quick, please, walk away from them," said Akira.

"Why? Perhaps they think I am a giant rat. They wouldn't be the first to mistake me for such. A writer must possess the ability to see his own physique, not to mention personality, in a true light."

The two men were saying something under their breath, and I asked Akira to translate for me.

"I cannot translate such things. I do not know those words. They are very—how you say?—naughty words."

"I see."

I walked to where the two men stood. They were actually taller than I, but the liquor in them had rendered their waists wobbly, their necks rubbery, and we saw eye to eye, four against one.

I could smell their breath. Rice wine gave off an entirely different stench when exhaled than did grape. Its foul chicken-coop nature delighted me no end. How would they respond to an Occidental's breath, my aromatic, sienna gums by now so thoroughly enameled in the resin of tobacco that the narrowed teeth protruded as if from the base of an antique comb?

I put my forefinger over my opened mouth and whispered, "Kay-gee-joh-gah-koo," the word for metaphysics. Nothing silences people like a bit of philosophy out of context.

The two of them stiffened their necks and stared at each other. Then they wormed their way around me, as if their entire bodies were now devoid of bones, making some comment to Akira before slithering, tripping every fifth or sixth step, away.

Akira and I walked on for a moment. He seemed to be turning over a profound thought in his mind.

"Those two men, very naughty. One call you crazy man. The other man says he does not understand red-hair foreigner talk. Did you speak English to them?"

"No. But it just as well might have been English. I do not have red hair, however."

"It does not matter. Red hair is a Japanese word for foreign barbarian. But old word, very old. Now we respect all foreign

Matsue

peoples. They have culture. We Japanese are the barbarians. We are all like those two men, drunk and very naughty."

A sumo wrestling bout was in progress in a small dirt ring. Nearby was pitched yet another tent with photographs pinned above the entrance. I went as close as I possibly could to see them. The barker smiled at me and I pressed two coins into his hand.

I had expected a sideshow of freaks such as those I had seen at fairs in America: a lady with a long beard, a man with pendulous breasts, a child the size of a fully grown adult. Inside the tent, on a high table, sat two people. The man had a scaly arm growing out from the center of his chest. With this hand he was amusing the few onlookers by scratching his forehead and picking his nose. Just after I arrived he lifted up the bottom of his robe to reveal his genitals. They looked perfectly normal, if rather small, until he took the tip of his penis in his third hand and raised the organ up. Underneath the penis were the lips of the female genitalia. I would not have seen it clearly had a metal and glass lantern not been trained directly on the area and had I not gone close in my inspection. Suddenly I noticed that others there—needless to say, all Japanese—were staring not at this rare, three-armed hermaphrodite, but at me. Was I a more bizarre and abnormal sight? Was it because I looked like an odd barbarian to them all? I had long accepted this definition of my appearance, long before coming to Japan. Here, at last, would I be seen for what I was? Perhaps I should quit my didactic calling and put out my perverse little shingle right here—the Metaphysical Cyclops of Matsue!

The man proceeded to insert his penis into his vagina, and I turned my attention to the woman. Presumably she was one. Would she open the front of her tattered grey kimono to reveal a handsome row of nipples, four say, or perhaps two or three rows, a regular dozen? Would she, like her double-sex partner, equally be able to go through the motions of intercourse by herself, the envy of more than one Englishman in our glorious Victorian era? I felt a hand on my shoulder. It was Akira's.

"We must go. Right now!" he said to me in a low voice.

"I want to see this first."

"No, please, professor. We are so late now already. Please. I am begging you."

A young man beside us said something in a hoarse tone.

"Yes, let's go," I said.

Outside I could see by Akira's expression that he was disgusted by the sideshow. He obviously could not understand why someone as distinguished as a teacher, a most respected profession in any Oriental society, would be attracted to the base and the grotesque.

"We Occidentals might truly be the barbarians, Akira. Do not forget it. Depravity is our coin, and it has always been so. What is actual deformity, eh? People living an upright life only torture themselves inwardly. It is better to be crooked on the outside. That may be the sign of a proper soul. The man whose followers I most profoundly hate, Jesus Christ, certainly live their lives according to outward respectability and inward perversity. It is the one hypocrisy that his followers—and I mean each and every one of the followers of Jesus Christ of the past nineteen centuries—have wiped from their minds. That is the nature of a following, I suppose—the possession of a shared and silent hypocrisy. A writer must ensure that he does not partake of this; he must, absolutely must, always siphon a wicked poison into his work, destroying his most ardent followers. Do not forget, Akira, that we Occidentals are totally depraved on the inside despite our demeanor of genteel, fine-lace etiquette. The thing I admire about the Japanese is that they accept their human nature for what it is. You are superior to us. I believe it."

We had reached the cracked wooden front steps of the temple's main building.

Matsue

"My father, who hated foreigners, will be waiting in paradise for you," said Akira. "He will accept only you, if you continue to talk like this."

"Why do you say that? Now it's I who do not understand you."

"Because we are mysterious people, yes, very mysterious, Mr. Hearn. We believe that no foreigner can ever understand us. If you realize this and still love us, you will be one of our new gods someday. Is this what you call a 'paradox'?"

"Are you mysterious too, Akira?"

Akira just smiled at me. It was the same smile I had seen on the face of every man and woman in this country. I was determined to get behind it.

A young apprentice monk with shaven head, wearing faded indigo robes, greeted us at the entryway. He bowed to the two of us, and we bowed back. He led us along a wide corridor and through a large tatami-matted room until we came to a stop at a closed door decorated with a painted peacock amid reeds. The grain of the wood showed through the paint. He called out to someone inside the room then slid the door open. We entered the room. Sitting in front of the alcove with a long-stemmed *kiseru* pipe in his right hand and his arm atop a cushioned elbow rest was a monk who must have been in his early sixties. The apprentice monk gestured that Akira and I should sit opposite his master.

"Please make yourselves comfortable," the old monk said in heavily accented English. "Sit with legs crossed. It is easier for you."

"I would like to do everything as the Japanese," I told him.

"That is impossible. Please."

He waved the hand that held the pipe up and down to instruct me not to remain on my knees. I sat and crossed my legs.

"You are late. But this does not bother me. My name is Chotaku Nagasawa. I am the monk of this temple."

"How do you do?"

"Akira has told me that you are a man of great learning."

"May I smoke my pipe too?"

"Yes," he said.

"He is my younger brother," said Akira, pointing to the apprentice monk who was sitting on his knees in a corner of the room.

I looked toward him and bowed my head slightly, but he remained rigid and did not blink. At that moment a beautiful girl, perhaps fourteen or fifteen, with a thin face, pale skin and exceedingly high, rounded eyebrows came into the room. She carried a tray made of intricately grained sienna-color wood. On the tray were tea and small cakes. I could not help but stare at her as she walked, shuffling over the mats, her bare feet making a conspicuous rustling noise. She kneeled beside the table, put the tray on the floor and proceeded to take each cup in its lacquered saucer and each cake in her hands, one by one. Her every motion was a picture of loveliness and grace. I was transfixed. After a long silence, with the tea and cakes in place in front of the three of us, she bowed with her fingertips together on the mat and said in English, "How do you do? My name is Yone."

While her head was still bowed Akira added, "She is my younger sister. She is only fifteen years old. Please be kind to her."

"Lafcadio Hearn. Very nice to meet you."

"If it were not for my generosity," said Nagasawa, "the brother would be a miserable beggar and the little sister would be forced to sell herself to men. Their father and their mother are dead, and they gave these children to my care. Akira was already studying, so he did not need me."

Matsue

"It was very kind of you," I said, taking the hot teacup from its saucer.

The old monk thrust his hand out. I put down my lighted pipe and took the *kiseru*, with its long stem and tiny bowl, from him, inhaling its sweet tobacco.

"The perfect pipe for us Japanese," he said. "We like only a very short and deep rest. We are satisfied with only a moment of silence."

"But the *kiseru* comes originally from Cambodia, or so I have read," I told him. "It is not truly Japanese."

Nagasawa burst into a hearty laugh. He stood up and went to the window.

"Come, look here, Mr. Hearn," he said.

I joined him at the window. Outside, a procession of the poorest peasants, dressed in rags, with only small striped cloth bags over their shoulders, could be seen going from one building on the temple grounds to another. The crowd of merrymakers, frantic in their movements among the stalls and amusements, formed a kind of whirling frame for this slowly moving grey line. It was dusk and there were even more people at the festival than before.

"They are very miserable pilgrims," said Nagasawa. "They come from deep in the countryside."

"How can they afford to come here, to take the time from their chores?" I asked.

"They cannot. But their faith is more important to them than their lives. After all, life is but a moment, yet the time in the other world lasts an eternity. We give them rice here. They must pay us only for the kindling to cook it."

"I have felt your religion to be superior to ours. Herbert Spencer teaches us that our religion has ceased to exist, that all we have left is the Great Doubt. This dispels all isms and leaves us with the true consolation of not knowing."

"Great doubt?" he said. "I do not understand this."

He turned to Akira for an explanation. Akira's younger brother stood up and walked to where we were. Was he going to explain this to his superior?

Nagasawa reached out his arm and struck his apprentice across the face, sending him to the floor.

"Do not dare approach me from the front, you idiot!" he screamed. "I apologize to you, Mr. Hearn, for the behavior of this young monk." Then he shouted something else to his apprentice.

"I am very sorry," said the young monk, putting his forehead against the mat.

"I must learn this from you if I am to understand you Occidentals," said Nagasawa. "The great doubt . . . I do not understand what there is that must be doubted." He laughed heartily as before, walking briskly out of the room, followed by his apprentice, who kept his head bowed the entire time. Once they were gone, Akira excused himself to go to the lavatory. Yone and I were left alone in the room. I looked outside once again at the drab pilgrims surrounded by whirling colors.

I had not realized at first that Yone had come beside me. Suddenly I could smell her. As I turned my face toward her, she slapped my cheek. This knocked my pipe from my mouth, but I managed to catch it in my cupped hands.

"I think you are sweet," she said in a soft deliberate voice, showing me her palm. In it was a large mosquito, the blood from its crushed body—my blood—forming a tiny irregular patch on the skin of her palm.

Yone closed her palm into a fist and smiled at me.

It was dark now. Akira had decided to stay at the temple. I stopped by the stall to pick up my one hundred paintings. The grounds were alight with torches and lanterns of every color and shape. The crowd of merrymakers was now crushing. I continually

Matsue

bumped into people as I pushed through it. I did not apologize nor did any one of them. I scratched my cheek, pulled down the brim of my hat and hurried away from the temple grounds.

I was sitting, at the end of fall, on the edge of my "wet verandah," with Edgar beside me, feeding two snakes that had come to frequent my garden since late August. Edgar merely watched the snakes, indifferent to their stalling and starting. I had turned forty in Japan. The snakes had no doubt come to remind me of this.

My first thought, some months before, upon seeing the statue of the Great Buddha in Kamakura, was that I should be grateful to die here, to mingle forever with the ghosts I found most companionable. The skeptic's perfect refuge is Japan. Then, someday, decades if not a century hence, I might count on being tossed a few dried morsels when entering, in some other guise—in my case a bat, rather than a snake, being appropriate—some poor outcaste's garden. He would be like me—I know that—a man who could live only on the periphery of his own society but who slipped, in a single smooth fall, into the center of this one. This would set the line of time curving once again, forming a circle, another's life, and so on and on.

Lovely. These snakes appealed to me. They made their way to my verandah without disturbing the bright orange leaves of the Japanese maple on the ground. I would somehow, I thought, have to find a way to describe the simple incongruity of this scene in English: the stillness that existed within movement. I had to discover the proper texture of language. We did not have it. Our English was too concrete, too intent on the composition of balance. In Japan two things which did not make sense together fit ideally into a whole. Pierre Loti was the only European writer who had understood this. But that was because the French language ventured on higher flights than ours. I thought, if only on my gravestone, my tall and narrow gravestone, I could write: "Here Lies the English-language Loti, Lafcadio Hearn, Who

Witnessed the Final Decade of Japan's Fateful Century." This epitaph would be in English at the very bottom of my stone. Its letters would be minuscule and an observer, perhaps one of my faithful "followers," would be obliged to get on hands and knees in the mud to read it. He might even have to scrape away the soaked soil or tenacious moss to see all of the words. At the top of the stone, just in case he might dare to overlook my message, I would engrave, in the fanciest arabesque of graven lettering: "Do Not Leave Before Reading the Fine Print at the Bottom."

I laughed at my own banal pomposity. Ah, the minor thoughts that occur to one while feeding two snakes! I waved my smoky pipe over their heads, a priest with his incense. This did not deter them. They merely lifted their heads and stared up at me. This would have scared any normal cat. But Edgar, like his eponym oblivious to terror, only tweaked his nose and licked a whisker. Wise cat. I wondered what great person he had been in a former lifetime—perhaps a persuasive Chinese religious leader or a renowned German etcher. I was certain that he had suffered a horrible and most excruciatingly painful death at the stake or, as was the custom, held down by four men and deftly castrated by a fifth, then disemboweled with the fine point of a sword and, while still conscious though hardly grateful for it, quartered. That must be what accounted for Edgar's blissful indifference to the world now.

The clock in my house struck eight times. There was a bitter chill in the air. It was time for me to light my lamps and get on with the work. The foxes of Japan fascinated me. Even the playing of a simple drum had the power to summon animals, the offspring of the dead fox whose skin now provided the sound, and make them weep. I was determined to create such reverberations with words. Some writers were content to speak to posterity. I was obsessed with words that reached back. By the time the clock had struck its eighth chime the snakes were gone, invisible under layers of fallen leaves.

I went into the house. It was now pitch dark. I had to grope my way through the room and up the steep staircase. Edgar remained

Matsue

where he was, eyes shut, blithe, dead to the world. The first thing that I did when seated with pen in hand was to describe his dream. I was afraid to stand up, go to the window and look down on him. I knew—yes, I was absolutely certain—that I would not see him there. But he remained there in my mind, dreaming of something that had happened, as I imagined it.

I was riding in a rickshaw toward the mountain that lay between my house and the seacoast. There were no trains in the Province of Izumo. In fact the nearest rail line was the one which went from Tokyo to Okayama. When I came to Matsue I had taken it as far as Himeji. There had followed a four-day rickshaw journey, stopping the nights at inns—rundown, if exquisitely neat shacks—and riding on a little steamboat from Yonago.

My poor runner this time was fifty if he was a day, with a head that was bald save for a tuft of long white hair above the nape of his neck, a wispy Oriental beard in reverse.

"I am sorry, I am sorry," I apologized to him. It was an unseasonably warm November's day, and the sweat poured off his head and down into the back of his brown padded jacket. He swiveled his head about, a smile dominating his face. It was obvious that he didn't understand a word of my English.

"*Tonbi no hane, tonbi no hane,*" he said through his teeth. I jotted these words down and checked them later in my dictionary. "Kite's wing . . ." Their meaning eluded me. Was this some sort of wise admonition by a simple man, a comment on work, manners or fate? Akira cleared it up for me by explaining that the runner had actually been attempting to speak English or what sounded to him like English. He had been trying to say, "Don't be in a hurry . . . tonbi no hane." "Or maybe he was having a joke at your expense," added Akira. "Maybe he was copying you. We Japanese are always best when copying. This is how we learn to act."

I sat perched on my rickshaw and looked up to the sky as we began to climb the steep slope. There were two enormous ravens facing each other, sitting atop two telegraph poles, probably about to contest territory. When we were equidistant from the poles I stood up in the moving rickshaw, took my hat off and waved it high above my head. Both ravens flew away. The runner threw me a swift sidelong glance, raising his eyebrows. He jerked his vehicle forward, and I fell back into my seat, barely managing to hold onto my hat.

We stopped at the top of the slope. The runner took out a heavy navy-and-white stitched cloth and wiped his entire head. The most magnificent sea I had ever seen in my life spread before me. It was nearing noon, and the water was a pale blue and willow green that nearly obliterated the line between it and the sky, the inner surface of a celadon bowl.

Once down at the shore I paid the runner fifteen sen and again apologized. This time he said nothing. He certainly would not have understood, at any rate, why someone would apologize for having allowed him to work. He took the money and bowed several times to me, pushing his open hand out as if to tell me to proceed to the pier.

A tour boat was moored beside the pier. The pier itself sat on pontoons and moved as one stepped onto it, an ingenious transition from dry land to open sea. I went onto the boat and sat on a bench to one side. Shortly after that a group of six young men, dressed in dapper European suits, came on, followed by two young women. I took particular note of one of the women, who had a squarish face and salmon-color skin, dark even by Japanese standards. She was talking to her friend, laughing and covering her mouth with her hand. I faced the sea and no one, perhaps out of native shyness, appeared to notice me.

The sea, which had been as smooth as celadon glaze when seen from the top of the hill, turned choppy beyond the promontory. The boat, by no means a large one, bobbed up and down. With each pitch my stomach, delicate since boyhood, was rolled in its pit, and I turned away from the rough culprit, burying my face in

Matsue

my hat. As I came up, from moment to moment, for air I glanced at my companions. The men were telling each other funny stories, passing around a *tokkuri* of rice wine. Each held a small empty cup in his hand. The two young women were huddled against the opposite side of the boat. With small chopsticks, no bigger than their hands, they were eating pickles from half-moon-shape lunch boxes poised on their laps. But such food and shared hilarity were the furthest things from my mind.

We rounded a rocky cape which was now tossing most decidedly upside-down. The sky, indeed, had become the sea. Lest I make my trusty hat even more aromatic than it already was, I quickly put my knees on the bench and my head over the side. I retched three times, but nothing came up. I held my hat behind my back. I retched again, wishing for some substance to leave me, to right this topsy-turvy vision. Nothing. I had had no breakfast to spill into the sea. I turned about and sat once again on the bench, my hat on my knees. It was then that I noticed the young woman—the one with the salmon-color skin—looking directly at me, holding one chopstick, with a pickle stuck on its tip, in the air. No doubt my Greek-Irish skin then had the hue not of fresh cod but of week-old mackerel. I lowered my gaze and stared into my hat.

We arrived at what appeared to be a deserted beach. All of the Japanese stepped off the boat before me. I was convinced that by standing up I would cause my stomach to yaw. The others were already walking toward a large cave some twenty to thirty yards from the shore. The boat's captain smiled and said to me in the Japanese that I was beginning to understand, "Please, sir, we have arrived." Gradually, and carefully, I stood. I breathed in the salt air fully, indicating to him with my raised hand that I was capable of alighting by myself. I walked slowly over the sand beside a flow of water which led from the sea into the cave. I bent down and put my finger in the water, tasting it. It was definitely seawater. The others, captain included, were looking in my direction, standing at the large mouth of the cave.

"Please come this way," the captain, acting as guide, said to us.

I followed them in. The interior was dark. We waited inside, near the mouth, as the captain and one of the young men fetched lanterns which had been sitting on shelves built into the cave walls. When each of us had his own, the captain lit them for us, instructing us to carry them low so as to illuminate our feet. The water in this little sea-river was calm.

At the back of the cave, where the water rippled to a stop, stood a large stone statue, perhaps fifteen feet tall. It had a smooth round head and a torso covered by what looked like a huge white bib. At the foot of the statue were countless piles of stones.

"This is the statue of Jizo," said the captain. "He protects dead children when they cross the river Sanzu and enter the other world."

I could understand his words well, for this was precisely the area of my interest and linguistic examination at that time. I may not have been able to specify clearly what variety of bean paste I preferred, but I could modestly converse on subjects concerning the afterlife and the deterioration of the one preceding it.

"Mothers who cannot produce milk," he continued, "pray to Jizo, and other mothers also come here to give their milk to their dead children."

As the Japanese in the group were listening intently to this explanation, I, as was my wont, wandered a short distance off. I was determined to examine this statue from all angles. On the wall behind it, attached by thick rusty nails driven into the dripping rock, were scores of votive tablets, most of them crudely executed. These tablets depicted women expressing milk from breasts the size of French balloons. The milk shot as broken dotted lines into little bowls or into the mouths of prostrate children. I held up my lantern to one tablet and pressed my eye virtually against it. Milk, expressed in a fine double curve from dark-brown nipples, flew through the air directly into the gaping mouth of a tiny skeleton—milk and bones, both white, the link between live mother

Matsue

and dead child. As I stepped back I inadvertently kicked over a stack of stones piled below this votive tablet. I looked back at the group. They were still giving their full attention to the captain's explanation, which was now dealing with the structure of the cave itself. I quickly put my lantern on the wet sand and began to restack the stones.

"You may notice little piles of rounded stones," said the captain, now turning his line of sight back to the foot of the statue, causing everyone to do likewise. "These piles are made by the dead children themselves in the middle of the night. These straw sandals which you see beside the statue of Jizo have been left for the children by fishermen. And look over here."

The group, led by the captain, started to come around the statue to where I was kneeling. I was trying frantically to make my fingers move nimbly, but the little round stones kept falling over each other, destroying my mound.

"Here are some marks in the sand. They are footprints."

I quickly took hold of my lantern and brought it around to a spot in front of me not far from the footprints, leaving the stones scattered behind me. The others in the group looked down at me. They no doubt thought that I was examining the footprints at close range.

"These are left by the dead children. They come to the Jizo at night, leaving their prints in a kind of procession."

Just then a low wave in the water of the little sea-river arrived at our feet. The others moved back rapidly but I, squatting down as I was, was unable to do so. The water washed over my shoes. When it receded I saw that the footprints had been washed entirely away.

"Do not worry," said the captain. "They will be back again tonight."

The people in the group stared in amazement at the clean surface of sand where there was now no trace whatsoever of the prints. Only the young woman with the salmon-color skin was looking at me—not at me, actually, but at my wet shoes.

I was first out of the cave, walking briskly toward the boat. I knew that I would not be sick on the return voyage. I stopped, for an instant, to take in the sea itself as it pounded the jagged rocks of the cape. The young woman brushed by me. Without so much as turning her head, she said, in Japanese, "Kindly excuse me."

I was not sick on the voyage, as I had predicted. That I had made an accurate prediction was all I remembered of my return.

The ginkgo tree in the schoolyard which had been, only a few days before, a fiery yellow was now bare, its last leaves taken by the gusts. Light showers, the so-called *shigure* of the season, were turning to snow. The students, whom I had been teaching since my arrival in the spring, had become quite accustomed to my queer appearance and ways. No doubt they would have been shocked to meet a normal Occidental, one who wore different clothes every day, one with seemingly conventional ideas. They would have thought him stupendously odd.

They rose and bowed as I took my place at the front of the classroom.

"First let us review your homework. Yanaka, can you name me please one famous English poet?"

Yanaka, a large oafish lad with ears that stuck out like the handles on a teapot, stood up, scratching the hair at the back of his head. He looked around the room as if he had not understood my question.

"Do you understand what I said?"

"Yes, sir."

"Good. Then answer please."

"*Eeto, eeto . . .*"

Matsue

He paused and looked around again, this time swaying his shoulders back and forth.

"Very well. At least speak English. *Eeto* in English is 'um.'"

"Um . . . um . . ."

Very good. Now the poet's name, please."

"*Eeto* . . . it is Tani-san."

"I beg your pardon?"

"Tani-san. This is the answer."

The other boys giggled.

"I do not understand. Tani-san is a Japanese name."

Then Yanaka, speaking Japanese, said that he thought the name of the English poet was Tani-san and that I had taught them that. The boys laughed more loudly.

Kobayashi, a frail and most clever young boy, stood up.

"May I please speak, teacher?" he asked.

"Yes, you may."

"Yanaka does not mean Tani-san. I think he wants to say Tennyson."

I held my lips tightly together but I must admit, I was tempted to join the boys in the round of guffaws.

"Thank you, Kobayashi. Is that so, Yanaka?"

"Yes, sir! Tani-san."

"Thank you. You may be seated now. Kobayashi, please remain standing. Would you please quote me something from Shakespeare?"

"Yes, teacher," he said, standing at attention. "To be or not to be."

He held his stance, looking wirier than ever.

"Thank you. You may be seated. And thank you also for not pronouncing 'to be' as the Japanese imperative for 'to fly,' namely, *tobe, tobe*."

The boys seemed to appreciate this remark, though all they did was nod. After that I read them children's verses written by several English poets. I knew that they could not grasp the meaning but felt that merely by listening to the cadences they might gain a sense of English stress and tone. The vocabulary could always be tacked on in adult life. In the last ten minutes of every class, I had for the past two months, for admittedly selfish reasons, made it a point to speak with them in Japanese. I walked up and down the aisles asking them to lower their defenses and talk to me as an equal, though I knew how very difficult this was for any Japanese.

"I would now like to ask you a question for myself," I said to them in my halting Japanese. "You are in a boat near Matsue and the boat one day goes . . . goes . . . um, under the water . . . um . . . Kobayashi?"

"Sinks."

"Thank you, yes, sinks. You are with your father and your wife. Whom would you save, I mean, save first?"

The boys exchanged nervous glances. They certainly did not want to offend their respected teacher with the arrogance of a strong opinion, yet they believed, as did the majority of their older countrymen, that Occidental influence should be confined largely to the scientific and industrial spheres and not so much as prick the surface of the moral.

Kobayashi stood.

"May I answer you, teacher?" he said in Japanese.

"Yes, please do."

"Please excuse my insolence, sir, but I will ask you first, please. Who would you save, teacher? Your father or your wife?"

Matsue

The boys froze, terrified at the possible consequences of a personal question asked by one of their number. Such a thing was unthinkable in a truly Japanese classroom. I, however, had encouraged such informality since the very beginning. Without it, I knew, my language could not be taught in its own social context. Mine was far from a truly Japanese classroom. What they could not know was that it was even farther from being a true classroom in any other country.

"A good question, Kobayashi," I said in Japanese. "Well, my real father did sink into the water and die. Also, I am not married, so . . ."

Two or three of the boys snickered.

"It's all right," I said. "But if I did have a wife and if my father were alive and . . . we were in a boat . . . I would save . . . my wife first."

There was dead silence in the room. Everyone looked at Kobayashi, the only boy on his feet. I myself was standing by the window, with my back to it. It was blindingly light outside, one of those rare occasions between fall and winter—as I was to witness in subsequent years—when the sun's rays seem to reach the air by means of a prism of magnified intensity. During those few hours of every year I was able to see with an uncanny clarity, the air in my midst acting as my individual lens. Seen from the inside of the room, my silhouetted face must have been a featureless shadow.

"Because I love her," I added.

It sounded strange in Japanese. I had used the words separately in Japanese before, but putting them together for the first time seemed somehow wrong, grammatically wrong. They did not sit well with each other, those words.

"Do Japanese find that bizarre?" I asked them all.

Kobayashi was urged to speak by the most subtle change in facial expressions directed at him by the other boys, expressions which I was now able to read with increasing accuracy.

"*Eeto . . . eeto . . .*" he said with uncharacteristic hesitancy.

"I am beginning to think that this equivalent of the humble 'um' is the most useful word in the Japanese language," I said, smiling and making all of them laugh.

"*Eeto . . .* I mean, no, sorry, teacher, in Japan this is not so," said Kobayashi, managing to look straight at me, though he could certainly not discern my features where I was standing. His face, which caught the light from the window, was illuminated and shadowless.

"In Japan," he continued, "you must love your parent more than anybody. To save your wife is . . . *fuketsu*."

I had not understood the last word of his statement.

"One moment please," I said, reverting to English and going to the front of the room where I kept a Japanese-English dictionary on my table. "Aha, I see. This word means 'unsavory,' 'impure.' Very difficult words for young boys. I think we shall leave it there today, unresolved. Unresolved questions are in their natural and final state. Oh dear, I am talking to myself. That is the last lesson for today, namely, the genuine teacher is one who talks primarily to himself."

The boys stood up, seemingly unperturbed by their confusion. They had come to expect as much from their teacher.

"The final word for today is 'moral.' 'Mo-ral,'" I said. "Please repeat that word, check it in your dictionaries tonight and think it over. Good day."

I walked up and down the aisles listening to them. It seemed to me that Yanaka was just saying *morau, morau* over and over again. This meant "I'll have that." Was he really so word-deaf or was he using these lessons to develop a fine cynic's sense. I hoped it was the latter.

Matsue

The boys remained standing and bowed. I took my dictionary and my hat from the table and left, not looking back at them or at the skeleton-branched tree in the yard.

The wind, blowing in fits, churned up circles of dust. I stopped, coughing, under the eaves of a soy sauce dealer's warehouse. It was then that I caught sight of Yone, Akira's sister, walking as rapidly as she could in her constraining kimono down the road. She turned a corner not twenty yards from where I was sheltering myself. I felt the impulse to follow her. I could always ask her about her brothers. But I noticed Chotaku Nagasawa, the old monk, striding down the same road and turning the very same corner as she. I followed them. As I turned the corner, Nagasawa entered an old rundown house. With some difficulty he slid the rickety door closed. I approached the house. The area, for some reason, seemed deserted. The sky was overcast, and I knew, by instinct rather than experience, that the first snow of winter would soon be upon us.

There was a single window in the house, covered only by a lattice of rotting wood and rice paper. The paper was relatively new, but, thanks to the wind, probably of that very day, there was a small slit in it. I peered in. Inside, on the one new tatami mat which was surrounded by dark-yellow worn old ones, Yone lay on her back in her kimono. The bottom half of the kimono was open, with the cloth neatly pushed back to each side. Nagasawa, wearing only his loincloth, was hunched over her, between her open legs. I could only see the nape of his neck from where I stood. His bald head had disappeared; his face, buried in her pubic hair, moving back and forth very slowly. His hands grasped her hips on both sides. Though he was lean and muscular for his age, a fold of fat hung down from the inside of his thighs. I could not see Yone's face.

I went around to the side. There was an exceedingly narrow space between the house and the one next to it. I squeezed along this space until I came to another window. This one had been papered long ago. The holes were such, however, that if I looked through one of them with my only seeing eye, the better part of my face would become visible to the two people in the room. I crouched down and, with the back and front of my body scraping against the sides of both houses, made my way to the far end of the window. I eased myself up and peeked through the hole.

Yone was now on her stomach with her legs spread wide apart. Her hips were narrow, and her buttocks small, those of a child. Nagasawa was on top of her, his penis thrusting rapidly forward, pushing her inch by inch along the tatami mat. His head was turned the other way. Yone was staring, as if possessed of two glass eyes, directly at me. I do not believe that she saw me. If she did, she did not, even in the most minute or subtle alteration of expression, permit me so much as to think it.

Rather than squeeze my way from out between the two houses, I crouched down and waited. The two of them left, Nagasawa first. It was nighttime before I so much as stirred. It felt strangely warm there, as if those two houses, with their coarse splintery wood, had been built decades ago solely to protect me, destined to be here, in this Japan, to encase and protect me against the coming seasons.

I was sitting as close as I could to my brazier, both palms flat against its smooth curved sides. I felt damned cold. The mercury did not plummet as it did in Ireland, but here it seemed colder altogether—Japan defying not only logic but the very elements as well. Akira was some moments late. Perhaps he was giving me a dose of my own medicine. No, he was too forthright for that. There was not a twisted bone in the young man's body. Meiji Japanese fit perfectly into the European suit at the close of my century. Deformity, of any variety, turned one into a misfit, pouring natural hatred, like burning oil, onto the scalp of its possessor. Conformity, on the other hand, was laudable, for it wedded the individual to the mass. In Japan nothing was worth achieving for oneself; everything was worth seeking for the nation. Imagine inviting an individual such as me into this!

Matsue

Akira arrived full of apologies. He had been held up at the temple, helping his brother with some matter. I sat him down by the brazier and went downstairs to the kitchen where, earlier, I had prepared a dish of food for the two of us.

"It is fish in a piquant tomato sauce," I told him, carrying the tray up the stairs, "though I have substituted ordinary pepper for cayenne."

"I have read about this to-ma-to sauce," he said.

I put the two plates down, and we began to eat, he with a knife and fork and I with chopsticks.

"It is a fish which the fishermen sold me after this morning's catch, a variety of sole, I believe. The poor men must go out even in this weather. It is like the Creoles make. I would like to make you something Greek, but I barely remember my Greek mother, and I cannot even presume to know how she would cook. I had a fiendish time getting the tomatoes, you know. I had them sent from Tokyo by Professor Chamberlain."

Akira had taken a bite of the sauce and was holding it in his mouth, staring down at the table without blinking.

"I am sorry, Akira. You do not seem to like it. I cannot tell myself if it is tasty or not, actually."

Akira swallowed his mouthful of sauce. We both noticed that the fish underneath had not been sufficiently cooked.

"It does not matter to me if it is tasty," said Akira. "This is your food. We must learn about it. Everything we do we must be learning. Tasty comes later."

He sliced off a piece of the glassy flesh and popped it into his mouth.

"Oh, please do not eat the fish if it is improperly cooked."

"This is no problem. We Japanese like raw fish, as you know. Perhaps this food you cook will someday be famous. It will be called Lafcadio Hearn's Sole."

I laughed.

"Oh, Akira, you do have a sense of humor after all."

"No, professor. I am being very serious."

He sawed down to and around the bone of the fish with the dull knife, pierced the entire fillet with his fork and put it in his mouth.

"I feel the way you do," I said. "Everything I do in Japan is a learning experience. I am a child once again, a child of forty."

"But there is nothing to learn here," Akira said, chewing vehemently, his mouth full of uncooked flesh.

"There is so much to learn here. There are the marvelous stories, the strange poetry, the curious traditions."

"These things are marvelous and strange and—how you say?—curious only because you are discovering them for your first time. We know them from birth. They are normal to us. And they are so old, just, uh, *meishin*, do you see?"

"You mean 'superstitions.'"

"Yes, that is it. Old women's and men's super . . . super. . . ."

". . .stitions."

"Yes, that is it. We want to be ridded of them, you see?"

"Very well," I said, lifting some fish and tomato sauce carefully to my mouth with my chopsticks, determined to be "Japanese." "Perhaps I will absorb these superstitions for you and whisk them away from Japan to America and Europe. Then someday, when you are ready to confront them again, you can always just borrow them back."

I put the fish between my teeth. It tasted rather good to me, though I was certainly an atrocious cook.

"You use chopsticks very well," said Akira.

"You use a knife and fork very well."

Matsue

"Oh, thank you so much, professor. Thank you so much."

After the meal, which we both finished with a cultural, if not culinary, gusto, Akira sat at my valise desk and read an article of mine about Japanese folklore recently published in America. Seeing that he was having much difficulty understanding it, I diverted his attention.

"You can see how much I read," I said, pointing to the high stacks of books lining the walls of the room.

"I wish that we had men in Japan with your practical learning, professor. We do not know how to use learning, only how to gather it."

"But that is all I do. I am certainly not practical. What good is knowledge, Akira, particularly knowledge about Japan? We humans owe more to our illusions than to our knowledge."

"We Japanese have lived that way for centuries," he said, closing the magazine. "That is why we must start over again."

I asked him to come to me beside the brazier. We sat together huddled against it, stoking the glowing charcoal. Neither of us said a word for some time. I felt very close to him. I knew that my station prevented him from allowing himself to feel the same camaraderie toward me.

Finally I spoke.

"Did you see your brother at the temple? How is he? Oh, and how is, uh, is, I mean, your little sister? What was her name? She is so frail."

"Yone."

"Yes. Yone."

"I did not see her at the temple this evening."

Akira picked up the metal chopstick-tongs and plunged them gently, over and over again, into the soft ash of the brazier.

I then changed the subject, asking him about the illness rumored to have come to Matsue.

"Is it cholera? One would expect cholera to visit in the warmer months. Professor Chamberlain wrote, when he sent my tomatoes, that there is a terrible outbreak of cholera in China just now."

Akira merely shook his head and said, "I do not know."

I offered to walk him home.

"Oh, please, professor, it is so cold now."

"Not to worry. The walk will wake me up. I must work when I get back. I am writing a book about Japan and can only work after midnight. Two o'clock, you know."

"Why two o'clock?"

"It is the time of the night that the ghosts in Japan come out, isn't it?"

"I would not know that kind of thing," said Akira, appearing for the first time a trifle annoyed.

We walked through the pitch dark streets of Matsue.

"That is the 'River of the Sky,'" he said, pointing upward.

"Ah, the Milky Way, eh?"

"Is that the English name? Milky Way. It is very beautiful, is it not?"

I looked up at the sky with him.

"The entire sky looks to me like a milky way," I said.

"I am sorry. Please forgive me," he said, bowing but continuing to walk.

"Think nothing of it, Akira. I prefer things to look that way. It stimulates my imagination."

We walked further on in silence.

Matsue

"It is I who should apologize to you, Akira. My Occidental dinner was an awful learning experience for you. You see, I do not have someone to cook for me."

"No, no, you are a wonderful cook."

"Ah, to possess such a trait as the ability to lie and pass it off as modesty. Which brings me to what I wanted to ask you tonight. I think I am becoming Japanese, mentioning what is on my mind only at the last minute. Do you remember me telling you about the boat ride I took to the cave with the large statue of Jizo?"

"Yes, of course I do."

"I am absolutely unable to forget the young woman I saw there. I described her to you. Did you make enquiries for me that day? She was, well, striking. That is to say, she struck me with her, well, forthright reticence, if that makes sense."

"Yes, I did make an enquiry."

"Did you find out who she was?"

We both stopped walking.

"Yes, I did."

"Who was she? You must tell me."

"Her name is Koizumi Setsu, or, I mean, Setsu is her Christian name and Koizumi is her family's name."

"Ko-i-zu-mi."

"Yes. That is it. Her ancestors are of a samurai family. She lives in her father's house."

"In Matsue?"

"Of course."

We began to stroll at the same time, walking in step. Before leaving him, I asked him once again about his brother and sister.

He nodded his head vigorously, said, "They are fine," and ran into the boarding house where he was renting a room.

Edgar did not return home until dawn. He simply slipped onto my lap as I fell asleep. My final notes of the night read, "Cats are superior to human beings," written three times beside a little sketch of Edgar.

In Japan, as everywhere, I most fear my blue devils, vengeful visitors against whose invasion of my entire body I have no natural resistance. I reason with them, but they refuse to be kept at bay. I cajole them and they smother me. I shudder in these wicked doldrums and can do nothing but wait—forlorn and sickened—until they release me and give me peace.

What if I were to marry? How could a woman possibly cope with me at such times, to find me in my study now uproariously gay, now weeping with a helpless rage? No woman could tolerate such a possessed man, no woman save a little Japanese one.

When I first arrived in Japan I was not unlike many an Occidental explorer, benefiting from Japanese naiveté and guileless reverence for everything un-Japanese. So long as Japan remained the kind of country that it was, absorbing culture from us in order to profit the nation, the great majority of Occidentals who came would have no commitment to the country, would be intent solely on channeling profit homeward. I was transformed. What had transformed me?

The glorious and immutable law of Japanese resignation, the decay which is seen as the true course of nature, the acceptance of the poverty of free will—that's what transformed me. How foolish we Europeans are in thinking that our monuments will last forever, that our beauty will long outlive the men who fashioned it. I found in Japan the only permanence that existed, the permanence of a profound belief in transience, the bright outline of the shadow, the only light remaining after the object that gave rise to it is gone. The light travels far, freely, even after the lamp that gave life to it has vanished.

Matsue

What woman could possibly understand this in me? In addition she would have to put up with burnt holes from my smoking in the cotton covers of my bedding. Only in a Japanese woman could such a combination of sympathies have been found. I would not be reformed, either in mind or in action.

A teacher of philosophy at the school had arranged a meeting for me with the father of the little woman. I had always been terrified of first meetings, particularly first meetings of a formal import. Most Japanese craved rituals, for they dictated how to act. I despised them, for they required me to be someone that I was not.

I was determined to present myself properly, to still my barely controlled temper and contain my blasted shyness lest my demeanor break its fragile bounds and cause me to rant. I stood outside the Koizumi residence, a finely kept traditional house. I held my hat in my hand. I would not speak Japanese to them for fear of sounding a fool. My pronounced vowels were, as Akira told me, "closer to what we think French sounds like than to Japanese."

Everyday words remained much of a mystery to me. I could understand them when spoken to me but had no ability to use them myself. My colleagues politely referred to my Japanese as "Hearn-san *kotoba*"—Mr. Hearn language.

"Excuse me," I said in a loud voice after having slid open the front door. A young maid arrived, sat on her knees and bowed her head to the floor. My shoes, new ones, bought for the occasion, were stiff and tight. As I took them off I stumbled, breaking my fall with my right hand on the raised floor of the entryway. Luckily this was not seen by the young maid.

The teacher of philosophy who had arranged the meeting was not there. This worried me. Indicating that I should sit with my back to the decorated alcove, the maid apologized, saying that the teacher had suddenly taken ill.

I was to meet my prospective bride's father alone. This I dreaded, and my entire body was instantly covered in a dappled film of perspiration. I considered leaving immediately. I could always say that I too had become ill. But the arrival of the father prevented this. He came into the room, sat at the other end of the low table and stared, unsmiling, at me. I felt faint. A fine groom I would make, losing consciousness at this first encounter, my heart pounding as one inside a Poe corpse, my face pale, awash with trickles of sweat, not an erudite and distinguished scholar but an ordinary Occidental ghost about to whisk his daughter eternally into an unrecognizable world. There was only one thing to do, for my own sake, and that was to talk. At least such a man could never fault my English. It was my sole weapon.

"Please excuse this sudden intrusion on your privacy, sir. I had expected my colleague to do the introducing, and I find it painful, indeed, to do it myself. I wish you to know that I come harboring no malicious intent whatsoever. That is to say, I would be honored if you would allow me to, to, um, accompany your daughter, Setsu, to a park, or, um, I . . . oh, I do not know if this is the proper Japanese custom, of course, rather than a park, I meant a temple or, perhaps, shrine. Where is Mrs. Koizumi? Perhaps it is proper that I greet her as well. Although I have spent some eight months in your exquisite country, sir, I must beg your forgiveness for my ignorance as to such customs as might relate to courtship, um, that is, I . . ."

I paused for a moment. The old man was still staring me in the face with a perfectly blank expression. I continued.

"I noticed, while walking through the corridor there what a fine and lovely inner garden—*naka-niwa*, is that correct?—which you, well, have. Our gardens in Europe boast grand fountains, et cetera, et cetera, but none can be as simple as one so totally without water, of only rock, pebble and, sometimes, yes, but not always, bushes. I admire your aesthetics. Well, I am sure that you have heard at least that about me. And these two swords on display in the alcove behind me—what wonderful specimens! Were these yours, sir? Such superb craftsmanship!"

Matsue

I twisted around and was about to touch the blade of one of the swords. The old man instantly sat up, the sinews of his neck becoming prominent, like cooking spits. I blinked my eye. For a moment his face looked to me like a chicken's. I swiftly took a handkerchief from my trouser pocket and wiped my face. Why had I delivered such an inane speech, as if I were a character not of Poe's creation but of Walter Scott's, or, measurably worse, James Fenimore Cooper's? Most of the time I was a successful parody of myself. Now I had managed to become a parody of an intellectual Western hick with a hackneyed background, and I loathed myself for it.

Setsu entered the room. She kneeled beside her father and bowed to me. She remained there, eyes averted downward the entire time. She was certainly no beauty, now that I could see her in her element, but I did not expect beauty. I expected only the taciturn ability in a woman to accept idiosyncrasy as commonplace. Any marriage to a man such as me would be grounded in that function.

I thanked the Koizumis for their hospitality and left, seen to the door by the young maid. I walked away from the house shivering. It had taken me the better part of two minutes to get my damned shoes on in the entryway. My feet ached from constricted bones, my ankles all but buckling. A light snow was falling. It stung my face. I was tired of catering alone to my own irascibility. It stood in my way. If nothing could be done about the blue devils, at least something would ameliorate my wretched loneliness. After all, I had lived with it by myself for forty years. I deserved a rest from it, if only to free myself for greater production.

A package arrived from America containing the galley proofs of a book of short stories I had written in New Orleans and on Martinique, and a magazine article about my first day in the Orient but no bank draft. These so-called friends and patrons of my art were proving less than worthless roustabouts when it came to money. Thanks to my handsome teacher's wage, I was able to live comfortably for the first time in my life, a welcome change to starvation, physical and spiritual. I decided to write letters to my erstwhile friends, these publishers and editors, telling them that no pool of blood or mountain of needles in hell promised sufficient hardship for them once they left this world. There was a personalized hell for each soul, and the one I envisaged for them was aswirl with foul poisonous ink and reams of suffocating pulp. A pleasant thought to warm the cockles of a writer's forsaken heart, eh? I was grateful to have the galley proofs, though they were useless to me at this distance. The book would be printed by the time they would reach the publisher by return post. I could, however, use their clean backs for new paper.

I spent the afternoon dozing, reviewing my life up to then. Were someone to someday write about it, there would be one thing inaccessible to him no matter how many details of a concrete nature could be salvaged. That one thing was my process of creation itself. No one can fathom how another's words flow from his fingers, how his organs dip into the massive red pool inside him, drenching themselves in the permanent liquid that eventually blackens into ink. I was finding an entirely new palette in my innards. Why should I be interested in anything that I wrote up to now, anything that came out of "Lafcadio Hearn before Japan"? It was not Lafcadio Hearn who wrote that, not the Lafcadio Hearn who reclines here on the tatami mats, slipping into and out of a sleep as if in and out of a pall of smoke.

I now see a face through that smoke. Whenever it is about to be obscured, a breeze reveals it once again to me. I run toward it cursing my eyesight, damning the child who threw the knotted rope and stick at my left eye, blinding it forever, imagining a refined hell for him, but all this rancor merely obscures the face. I concentrate on it as hard as I have concentrated on anything. The face comes closer. Its eyes peer at me. I recognize first the eyes, then the shape of the face, the whiteness of the cheeks, the long soft neck . . . Yone's.

Matsue

The front door rattled open, and my head jerked up from the mat. The clock attached to the wooden pillar built into the middle of the wall showed 6:05. It was dark outside, with no snow. I had spent the entire afternoon lying there, drifting in and out of a dream. I stood, called out, "Come on up," and adjusted my heavy kimono and the long woolen underwear beneath it.

Akira and his younger brother came up the stairs. I had been expecting them but, unfortunately, had not, as I had planned, gone out to get something for them to eat. All I had on hand was some dried squid and rice crackers. But I had had several cases of beer delivered in the morning and left them on the verandah to chill. I went to the window. Edgar, rather than come inside, was sitting between the two crates, just as I had once, between two old wooden houses.

I opened three bottles of beer and offered the men squid and crackers. Akira asked me if I had met the father of Miss Koizumi.

"Oh, yes," I replied. "A most charming man."

The front door slid open again and, puzzled, I looked at the two of them. We heard it close, followed by the sound of footsteps coming up the stairs. Chotaku Nagasawa appeared at the door of the upstairs room.

"You will please excuse me," he said. "My young disciple told me where he was going. I thought it will be the chance to see the learned Professor Hearn once again."

Akira's brother fixed his eyes directly downward.

"Welcome, Nagasawa-san," I said. "You will have to be content with beer and a few strings of dried squid, I am afraid."

"Beer? Nothing can make me more content. We Japanese priests are not like your ones. We do not let our belief stand in the way of our pleasures."

He laughed as he held an empty glass in his hand.

"We are not all that bound," I said to him, pouring beer into his glass. "Only the Protestants, you see. They deny themselves. The Catholics give in to their sins and still go to heaven so long as they confess them before their last moments on Earth."

"Ah, some room for your great doubt, then?"

He laughed again, even more loudly, and drank half the beer in his glass.

"They give in to sins?" he added. "All of their sins, Professor Hearn? Who chooses which sins are forgivable and which are not?"

I started to pour beer for myself, but Akira took the bottle from my hand and poured for me, insisting that I raise my glass.

"I would not know that," I said. "I am neither Protestant nor Catholic."

"What are you then?"

"I am a Buddhist, like you."

"Like me?" he said, finishing his beer and offering the glass to me. "Take it, please."

"It is a Japanese custom," said Akira. "You drink out of the glass of the other person."

I held the monk's glass as he poured for me.

"You must drink it to the bottom," he said, filling the glass.

I drank the beer and returned the glass to him. He held it up as I filled it.

"Very good, Professor Hearn. Very good," he said, smiling at me. "But of course, you foreigners will never truly understand Japan, only the outer things, no matter how long you stay here, even if you become Buddhist yourself, even if you become Japanese yourself, even if you take a Japanese wife."

"There is nothing so rewarding, Nagasawa-san, as attempting something which all people consider impossible. Perhaps I was a

Matsue

Japanese in a former life and you were an American, perhaps even a Protestant preacher in Pennsylvania or Massachusetts. Who knows? Do you know?"

"Aha, very interesting, is it not?" he said to Akira's younger brother who, still facing downward, had not so much as touched his beer.

"You may have read much about our faith, Professor Hearn, but you cannot understand it. Take cats. They are, how do you say, wiry beasts. Do you say? Wiry and ungrateful?"

"I think you must mean 'wily.'"

"Oh, yes, you must forgive my pronunciation. It too is Japanese."

"Not so bad as Mr. Hearn language," I said. "But I do not agree with you about the cats."

"You see? You do not think as we do, as a Japanese. Cats and poisonous snakes did not weep at Buddha's death. Therefore they cannot go to Paradise. They must go to Hell. It is not like with your religions. It does not help a cat or a man to confess sin. It does not matter what the individual thinks about his actions, because there is no such thing as an individual."

"Well, I shall no doubt be there with them."

"Eh?"

"With the cats. In hell. I wonder what my hell will look like?"

"You can learn something from us, Professor Hearn. We worship many gods, but only when they are useful to us. Many Japanese worship the god of Occidental civilization now. I do not disagree with this. It is only one more god for us with all of our other ones. We find it suitable to worship what we need—how do you say?—for the time being?"

"Yes. For the time being."

"Thank you. For the time being. Excellent. Now, please pour me more beer. It makes my head very clear."

We sat and drank in silence for some minutes. I urged Akira's brother to drink out of my glass. This brought him, temporarily, out of himself. I was feeling rather drunk. The monk had a fiery-red face. He clenched and unclenched his teeth. Akira sat beside a bookshelf, leafing through an American magazine. His brother leaned against the window with Edgar, purring, on his lap. They all looked so distinct to me, and I could see what their essence was in perfect detail. I must, I thought, find the words from that damned blackening pool to describe them.

"You Occidentals are too worried about the fight between the flesh and the soul," said the monk. "Why worry over it, eh?"

"Yes, I have learned since coming to this country that a Japanese can commit a sin without being burdened with guilt on his conscience. The conscience is a kind of ledger, is it not? A payment to the temple cancels the liability of a sin?"

"I do not fully understand your question, but I think that you do know much about us. Lust, do you say? Lust is natural, no? Any religion that does not see this ignores the way humans truly are made."

"I agree with that," I said. "But how can you shut your eyes to misery around you while satisfying your own lust? Is that the modern Japanese religion?"

He now laughed uproariously.

"We were much worse in our history. You have come at a time when we are trying to act civilized to show the outside world we can be like the white peoples. But it was you who are blind to misery. You burned people at the stick during the Acquisition."

"It was at the *stake*, and during the *Inquisition*. But you are right, Nagasawa-san. 'Acquisition' may be the more proper word to describe Occidental philosophy. I suppose that I am seeking here something which is lost or never existed in my own culture.

Matsue

Why should I not? Why should I not look for an ideal here? I do not care what you do in your life. It is different from mine. I do not care how you exclude me from your Japan. I can just as easily exclude you from mine, from my Japan."

"From *your* Japan?"

The monk seemed not to understand what I could possibly have meant by this. We were both drunk. I doubted whether he was listening to me at all. Even when sober, discussion with a Japanese on abstract themes was, at best, a game of intellectual hide-and-seek.

We had emptied more than a dozen bottles. The three Japanese had not touched one string of my dried squid or a single rice cracker. I lay on my side with my head in my palm. The monk stood up, screaming at Akira's younger brother.

"You stand when I stand!"

The young man did not stand. He merely sat, legs crossed, by the window, petting Edgar. The monk walked over to him and kicked his leg. His toes struck Edgar's ear. Edgar jumped out of the brother's lap, giving off a sharp yelp.

"Professor Hearn, are you awake?" asked the monk.

"Yes," I said, looking up at him and seeing three or four bleary round images against the matching grain of ceiling planks.

"I apologize for injuring your cat. I will pay to have it put down if it becomes necessary."

He exited. I blacked out. When I awoke it was half past two in the morning. The room was freezing cold. I had never felt so miserable since coming here. This time I had no one to blame but myself. I had, thanks to the old Japanese monk, become my own blue devil. Yet that realization was to free me to enter into the most startling process of discovery of my lifetime.

Roger Pulvers

I was not to remain long in Matsue. From the spring of '91 I transferred to Kumamoto on the island of Kyushu, together with my wife, Setsu. The wedding had been set on a day in January. Who would have thought that the short-statured, hirsute and homely boy, having received the wishful Christian prayers of the relatives and teachers who were his begrudging wardens, would someday marry, not under the watchful and all-seeing eye of the Great White Bearded Father but of the invisible myriads of shifting Shinto gods?

The fact was that I fit into this society, with all of its contradictions tacked on and its cheap yet so-dearly-believed-in sentimental effects, as I had not into any other. I could not have been a Creole despite my dark skin and committed Francophilia. I could not have truly joined the West Indians. To them I was an enigma with my nighttime reading and my winded arguments. As for America, I found New York City to be too hectic to nurture a contemplative culture—the only genuine kind—and too swarming with petty *ad hominem* maledictions to allow sufficient freedom to create the abstract. And the materialism of a town like Cincinnati overwhelmed even the least tender soul. I carried away from America nothing except an image of its monuments and its idols, the idea of America being far superior to its realities.

No one truly understood Japan, or so I was told repeatedly. Perhaps I, a black heron, free from attachment to any particular nation or culture, was the only person who could fathom its depths and rise up once more into the air to tell the world what I had witnessed. This I set as my task, as the first year of my life in Japan, 1890, was drawing to a close. I would not, I vowed, like other writers doomed to forget themselves in the comfort of expatriate life, lose my original gift here; but rather I would reinvent it and allow it to assume a valid and permanent Japanese guise. I would express my gift in every Japanese trapping. The words that I created here would be neither Japanese nor English. They would be in-between words, grasped only by those readers who abandoned their own stance and joined me, from one side or the other, in the whirlpool of space that only I, at least for the time being, occupied. Only I! Only I! And if no one from either side made the effort to slip toward me? I would gladly suffocate in the space deprived of air by my own agitation.

The five days from New Year's Eve till the fourth of January were blissfully solitary. I had no one to keep me company but Edgar. The little town all but closed down. Not that it was much of a change from other times. Colleagues, friends such as I had, even stray acquaintances of a single chance meeting were ensconced in their flimsy houses, celebrating the good fortune of being alive to see the dawning of the year 1891. But Edgar's life changed little. His *copains* recognized no national holiday. They met at their usual high places, the desolate scenes below merely encouraging them to scour.

The Japanese stopped work only twice during the year: at the Bon Festival of the Dead in the middle of July and at the New Year. Though they managed to get drunk at these times like upstanding working people in any country, one did not see staggering and unruly individuals on the streets. All vice was permitted in Japan so long as it was kept strictly private. No sin, however trivial, however easily forgiven for its scale, was tolerated if exposed.

Edgar and I took only one walk during our five-day retreat, and that was to the house where I saw Yone. I might have thoroughly despised Chotaku Nagasawa for his lecherous crime against the young girl. I might have been envious for not being able to absorb that innocence myself, to feel for long moments the hand that gently slapped my face, to look at close range at the lips that pronounced me "sweet." Edgar entered the house as if it were his territory. He sat exactly on the spot where Yone had lain on her back and looked at me with the same glassy eyes as she had. As we meandered home, I felt an indescribable warmth inside me, as when I considered myself above greed and the desires of other people, aloof from all humanity.

On the day before the wedding, Akira and I took a walk in the mountainous area some miles from Matsue. We stayed on the path by the foot of the mountain where it was relatively warm. It was one of those false springs in mid-January which I was to experience in later years in Japan. Akira asked me if I was happy to be married and if I wanted to have children. I answered married yes, children no. Marriage would provide stability to my life. Unlike many French writers, I had always craved a stable domesticity where my meals were provided regularly and someone would look after my dreaded personal needs. As for children, I loved their audience, their stares and questions. "But I do not want others, not even my own children, to be dependent on me," I told him. I had had enough of being dependent, totally, helplessly, humiliatingly dependent, when I was a child and a young man. It was just such dependence which forced me in upon myself, making me excruciatingly shy and reliant on my fantasies for comfort.

As I was telling Akira this, a number of rather large rocks became dislodged on the side of the mountain's wall above him as he was walking several feet ahead of me. Noticing this I rushed to him and pushed him away and down, jumping off the side of the path myself. We were both missed by the rocks, which might have done considerable injury to Akira, if not killed him. Akira, for an instant, was perplexed, glaring at me from the ground. Then he took in the entire incident and, getting on his hands and knees, bowed to me, thanking me profusely for saving his life.

When we stood, we both realized that we were hurt, ironically both in the same place, the right wrist. As it turned out, neither of us had broken our wrist, only severely bruised and strained it. But from then on we had another bond of experience. And whenever we met we would shake hands with our left hand. We called this our "symbolic gesture."

It snowed heavily on the day of my wedding. Setsu, my bride, and I wore the traditional attire for a Shinto wedding. A thick band covered the horns of jealousy on her head—in Japan it was the women, not the men, who were possessed of jealousy, being

Matsue

the sole prejudice in this country which I never was able to understand—and tucked in her obi, she carried a convenient stiletto, to do away with herself readily and honorably if her husband died. This I understood with no trouble at all. After the ceremony we walked along the path between towering cryptomeria trees, followed by my parents-in-law. Being so much older than my bride, I had difficulty looking upon them as parents. We could barely understand each other. Yet perhaps that was the ideal state of parent-child. Were I miraculously to find my mother and were she walking here in this cold and rigid atmosphere, so foreign to her, I would have prostrated myself on the snow before her. We too would hardly have been able to communicate with each other clearly, thanks to the barrier of years and language. She had been an ideal mother for me, for I had been able to bow before her all my life with a flawless worship, never having known her consciously in the flesh.

The snow that had accumulated on the branches fell with a loud thud throughout the precinct. Akira came running through the torii gate holding the skirt of his formal dress up to his shins. I had expected him at the wedding, but he had not appeared. We waited as he approached. He came to me and told me to follow him out of the precinct of the shrine. I sensed a terror in his voice. We ran some distance toward the torii before I stopped to look back. My bride and her family were standing stiff and still, no doubt nonplused at the behavior of this barbarian groom. It would not be the last time that I would confound my poor wife with my impetuous behavior. Perhaps she was lucky to experience it so soon.

Akira led me to the town hospital. No one seemed to take notice of our formal dress. The hospital itself was exceedingly primitive, with no modern facilities that, as I had read, Japan boasted in such institutions in its larger cities. It was as if this place were still held in the isolation of Japan's recent past. Patients lay on the floor on thin mats, one virtually on top of the next. They were writhing and defecating, shrouding the air with stench. I did not mind this. I walked slowly down the center aisle in the windowless room as the sick people, unmoving, stared at me in my neatly creased formal kimono.

Akira, ahead of me, indicated that I should follow him into an adjoining room. This room had beds placed far enough away from each other to allow people to visit with patients. He whispered into my ear as I stood beside him.

"Do not mention the word *cholera*."

In the bed, covered up to his chin by a blanket inside a folded sheet, was Akira's younger brother. I looked down at him. He barely managed to open his eyes, tiny strips of black paper on edge. I took his hand and squeezed it, though Akira visibly disapproved of this gesture. His brother gave me a faint smile, saying something softly to me. I put my ear next to his lips. His words came out with no more force than a breath.

"O-me-de-to . . . congratulations," he said, pausing to close his eyes then adding in English, "I wish you happiness, Hearn-*sensei*."

"Do not call me *sensei* . . . teacher," I said to him, holding his hand to my chest. "Call me *o-nii-san* . . . elder brother."

He closed his eyes, but the smile did not leave his lips.

"When you get well, come to see Edgar again," I told him, stepping back. "He misses you. You are two kindred souls."

I turned around to look at Akira and noticed that Yone was standing behind him. She wore a white nurse's smock. It was strange for me to see her there, with both of us in a kind of uniform. I could feel my cheeks flushing. Unlike other Japanese women, she did not look away from me but rather straight into my eye. The thought occurred to me that I should have married her, despite the twenty-six-year gap in our ages. But it did not weigh heavily on me. My passion for women lay in how free they left me to pursue myself. I saw a consuming passion as the artist's enemy. He may write about it, praise it, sing hymns to its fire, but he is deceiving himself if he believes that his true motivation comes from it. If I had allowed passionate love to take me for an instant and feel its spark—or given myself over to it for longer—the only possible result would have been enslavement in a blackened sterile room for all eternity.

I made my way alone through another room that had beds placed against each other. As I neared the back door of the building, I heard a voice calling to me in English from behind. I turned around but could not see where it had come from.

"Professor Hearn. Over here," said the voice.

I half-turned again to see Kobayashi, my star pupil, lying under a heavy blanket. He was shivering through his teeth, clenching them to appear unperturbed by his fever. His face was chalky, his eyes bloodshot.

"When this happens to people, all of the differences between them disappear. Is that not so? Are we both equal now, *sensei*?" he said. "To be or not to be?"

"When what happens?"

I feigned ignorance of his disease.

"Professor Hearn, if I survive this, I shall become a teacher of English like you or perhaps a writer like you. That is what I want. You are my wonderful teacher, Hearn-*sensei*."

"You get better," I said. "You must get better. For Japan."

"Thank you," he said, closing his eyes.

Among my students it was Kobayashi alone, I had to admit, for whom I had affection. What use the others would find for a scant knowledge of my language I did not profess to know, neither then nor now. My language, like my civilization, was an outfitter's suit to cover their skin. The fact that one wore it and that it fit was the only thing important to them. They need not have questioned its meaning for them as individuals. If the suit fits others, wear it yourself—such was the national motto of Meiji Japan.

Roger Pulvers

Do not decide anything yourself. Do not bring your own powers of concentration to bear. Do not revere that which is inside you inherently, only that which can be acquired as mock-Occidentals.

Other foreign visitors lived in Tokyo, Yokohama or Kobe. This gave them a most untrue picture of Japan, one where the superficies had already replaced the core. In Matsue I had seen the core exposed, in places like a temple festival celebrated by miserable peasants, a beautiful cave for the midnight dead and a hospital reeking of incurable illness and eyes that will never unfix their gaze.

The contradictions in me, coexisting in an ideally irresolvable state, were mirrored in that old coastal town on the Sea of Japan. The people living in Japan who shared my so-called birthright were preoccupied with what was only a false illusion of harmony. No amount of time spent here would ever be enough for them to see straight into the core.

The thing I recalled most vividly from the funeral was the intense cold, of a kind that I had not experienced before. The Japanese cold seeped into one gradually, leaving one defenseless to root it out. The air differed in this way from the European or American. The rain, wind, heat and cold enveloped the body and then pierced it, growing down into it. One could not be a mere observer of these elements; one became a part of them despite oneself. That is why the Japanese were the better examiners of the air. They attacked the problem by studying themselves. We Occidentals, armed with the Greek and Latin of our logic, at best *described* nature. We did not become a part of it, with all the pain this entailed, in order to know it.

The late-January cold, in the form of mist, settled on me. I could not move. My good eye throbbed as if filled with blood. I sat still with the few others in the open temple chamber. Smoke from incense rose and dispersed. I followed it carefully. The droning of the sutra, chanted by Chotaku Nagasawa, sounded in my ears

Matsue

like a piece of novel American machinery. There were no pauses, and my impression, sitting stiffly nearby—my bones so rigid that the slightest action would certainly have splintered them into thorns—was that this noise was destined to become louder and louder, never ceasing, until all of the people in the country, save me, would be forced to cover their ears and flee.

Akira and Yone sat on either side of the old monk, somewhat behind him. Other apprentice monks were also present. Akira's little brother had died in his eighteenth year. Akira picked up the box containing the urn with his ashes inside, wrapped it in a large white cloth and carried it outside. Yone followed him. Nagasawa stood and retreated into an inner room off a corridor, leading a procession of his apprentices. I remained seated, facing the altar, my back perfectly straight, frozen stiff by the unceasing sounds that filled the air.

An hour later, toward evening, I saw Akira sitting on a wooden plank outside. The plank was drawn over two rocks below a red pine. The box with his brother's ashes inside was now hanging from his neck on a white silk ribbon. Yone was nowhere to be seen. It was he who started to speak. I would have preferred to have said nothing.

"This is the end of my family. Yone was permitted to stay at the temple only through the goodwill of Chotaku Nagasawa. Now that my brother is dead, Yone will be forced out."

For some reason I turned away from him, as if to search the temple grounds for something, perhaps the sight of people. But we were the only two people there. Akira was shivering, barely managing to hold back his tears.

"Can she not live with you?" I asked.

"She cannot. I have only enough money for one small room."

"Perhaps I can take her in, Akira."

Such generosity, I had to admit, was not my strong point, though I had been, on innumerable occasions, in innumerable places, on the receiving end of it.

"Thank you, Mr. Hearn. But this is impossible. You are married now. Your obligation is only to your wife and family. There is nowhere. Japanese are very bad. They do not help strangers. This is why your civilization is better. You have Christianity. You have a *magokoro*, a true pure heart."

I felt it improper to argue at that time with Akira. I left him there and went home.

These details were reconstructed after a prodigious concentration on my part. The memory of the cold and the sound obliterating everything else, except one face, persisted. As I walked, that one face, Yone's, appeared before me. The face itself was composed of soft snow, and it moved as I moved, ahead of me, at an unchanging distance from me, a white shadow that was as much a part of me as it was of the congealed air.

Setsu poured me hot saké.

"I hope that it is the proper temperature," she said.

I sipped it.

"Very hot. Very good."

I could never hope that she would speak English. My miserable Japanese was to set the level of communication for both of us. She filled my tiny cup again.

"I ought not to drink too much," I said to her, slipping into English.

She gave me a puzzled look. I took her hand and kissed the back of it. She looked away and, with her free hand, picked up an American magazine.

"I wish that I could read what you write," she said.

Matsue

"It is of no importance," I said, once again in English.

She put the magazine back on the tatami mat. I inched myself toward her until my knees were touching her. Her head was bowed so low that her chin was touching her chest. I reached around to her back and started to untie her obi. Had I known the extent of training and practice it takes to learn to tie these cummerbunds, I would have bowed to my young wife then and there on my hands and knees and begged her to do it herself. I was to become a self-styled master of things Japanese over the coming years, but this mastery was limited strictly to the abstract, the philosophical and the aesthetic. When it came to knots, I was a hopeless novice.

"Please help me," I said to her in Japanese.

"You must have *gaman*," she replied.

"What is that? Nimble fingers?" This was in English. It was only the first of many quips I was to make during the span of our marriage, more often than not for my own amusement.

"*Gaman*? It is, well, *gaman*. Use your dictionary. It is there, by the lamp."

People who did not know foreign languages seemed to think that repetition of the mysterious word was sufficient to clarify its meaning. I was not about to get up at that moment. I learned later from my dictionary that *gaman* meant "patience, endurance, perseverance."

I fiddled further with the knot without result. I slid my hand along her leg, from her ankle to her thigh. She wriggled back, my hand falling off her thigh but still inside her kimono. She untied the string fastening the obi at the front then undid the knot in back. The obi fell to the mat. With one hand I opened the front of her kimono to reveal yet another kimono underneath. This too was tied firmly with an obi. I was beginning to think that *gaman* was the key to understanding a great many points of the Japanese sensibility, a sensibility founded not in an affluence of emotions but rather in their paucity—or absence. In Japan one's cup did not runneth over. One was lucky—and content—to get a few drops to cover the bottom.

When Setsu was finally naked I stood her up in front of me and examined her thoroughly with my magnifying glass. What fascinated me more than anything was the bone structure, so different from the Greek, and the way the hair lay over the body, more willowy and clinging, neatly laid down as if combed, not resisting the skin in clumps as it did with us. Her pubic hair, in particular, was silky and straight, curving only as her body curved inward. I put my glass very close to it, and the smell brought me back instantly to my New Orleans kitchen, with full-bloods, mulattoes, quadroons and octoroons rushing about, wafting myriad scents under my ample nose—the fresh celery, the hairy okra, the pigs' feet fried in batter, oysters stewed with milk, and, oh, that blackberry pie! Was this so strange a thing to daydream about at such a time? The man who would think so could never have traveled any true distance in his life. And the man who could keep his mind fixed on a single prolonged sexual event without associations crisscrossing his senses lacked the writer's susceptibility.

"You have tiny bumps on your hips," I said to Setsu in Japanese.

"I am freezing!" she said, not even looking down at me.

I was training myself to be oblivious to the cold, and it had made me neglectful of vulnerability toward it in others. I crawled to our heavy futon bedding and slipped inside, opening the top quilt to invite her to join me. As I made love to her I became aware of a sheet of pale light on the window, thanks to moonlight reflecting off an even-textured dusting of snow on the old slivered wood of my verandah. Perhaps it was that reflected light which caused me to feel an ecstatic sensation piercing me for an instant, like a warm needle sticking not into my groin but through my wide-open globe-like eye. This sensation lasted for five or six seconds, in spurts, then was gone. By the time it had passed into my brain and through me, I was fast asleep.

The supreme authority in the prefecture, Governor Yasusada Koteda, was an admirable man, shunning obsequious mimicry of everything Occidental and resisting its confusion. He had revived sword-fighting and spear-throwing contests, encouraging preservation of the old martial spirit. The schoolchildren were miserably overworked with studies of things alien, and to what end? They had no time to rest the spirit, sacrificing it in the name of the public lust for so-called modernization. I often felt as if I myself were, willy-nilly, an instrument of that lust. I envied my friend Professor Chamberlain in Tokyo. He taught Japanese to the Japanese. I was obliged to teach them English.

I was at home in the frost of words and silences. The formality of Japan suited me down to the ground. In America my shyness had been my enemy, the butt of wisecracks and ill-intentioned swipes. Here it was not only accepted but admired. To be withdrawn was a virtue. The tall, hard wooden pillow on which I rested my head every night was comfortable, but the food, I confess, I considered absurdly bland. It did not sufficiently nourish me; and I presented my wife and kitchen servant with a new copy of *Eliza Acton's Recipe Book*. They studied it for one hour each day and tried to prepare new dishes for my dinners. But everything came out the same, devoid of any piquancy. I longed to take a trip to French Indochina, if for no other reason than to smell real food once again.

Taking Akira with me as my interpreter I visited my father-in-law's house on a gray afternoon in late January. Setsu had returned to her parents' home that morning in order to help her mother prepare a meal for me, her father and grandfather. The two men talked continuously, telling me stories and legends of the Izumo region. I had asked them to concentrate in particular on the bizarre, the uncanny and the terror-inspiring. This was not difficult.

Virtually all Japanese stories and legends were bizarre, uncanny and terror-inspiring. Akira seemed a trifle embarrassed.

"This is all very old story, Hearn-*sensei*," he said. "We do not believe this anymore. We are humble because we have *bunmei kaika*, enlightenment and civi . . . civilization—you see, I can say the word now—from you and your people."

"The characters in these stories are my kin, Akira."

I continued to make notes of what I was told by my wife's father and grandfather, well into that night. Houghton, Mifflin and Company had accepted the manuscript of my first book about Japan, *Glimpses of Unfamiliar Japan*, but I was determined to send them two more chapters, even if it led to an eventual rejection. My book had to be balanced in favor of the real Japan. Books about Japan were coming out in the United States at the rate of one every month. It was important that I showed people, with a final eye to my Japanese audience, that Japan must be cured of the debilitating Occidental infection. Before setting foot in Japan I had used words as mere ornaments, juxtaposing gaudy color beside gaudy color, as if richness in tone were enhanced by loudness alone. Now I wanted to write in English as if I were writing in Japanese, to be ruthlessly spare, to inhale the full Japanese air and, exhaling, somehow thin it out, transforming a storm into the least-felt breeze. By doing so I would no doubt have been misunderstood by both Americans and Japanese for a time. No Japanese was content to be readily understood. It was the blatant sign, if not proof itself, of facileness. Any American editor who balked at this would incur *my* rejection.

I heard that day about the *kitsune*, the Japanese fox, and about Yuki-Onna, the mysterious snow woman whose white face scares to death those who venture out into winter alone. Setsu's grandfather was born at the beginning of the nineteenth century. His ways had not changed with the times, and his spirit had not succumbed to their corruption. Her father was equally uncompromising. He acted toward her as he had before she was married.

Matsue

He shouted orders of food and drink. He criticized her for her lack of promptness when she brought them. Had she no respect for the three men in her life: grandfather, father and husband? She replied with a bow and a "Yes, father," before rejoining her mother and her servant in the kitchen.

I wrote my two chapters, not finishing until well past three in the morning. After that I hungered for an omelet. Neither my wife nor the kitchen servant had returned. I opened *Eliza Acton's Recipe Book* and tried to follow the instructions. But I could not understand them. My mind had become unaccustomed to such step-by-step English. This pleased me no end. Did it mean that my mind was entering a different dimension, one more suited to following my mysterious spirits than the simple steps necessary to cook an egg? The cold stove on which lay two broken bloody eggs, the white cover of cloud plastered to the ceiling, thanks to the haze in my eye, and Edgar assiduously licking his paw then abruptly looking straight through me—that was what I had been waiting for all my life.

The day I left Matsue for good was a bright and windy one. I made the mistake of opening the upstairs windows fully, and the bulk of my papers were swept over the floor in the cross-breeze. I could hear Setsu downstairs packing the crockery and warning Edgar to get out of her way. I got down on my hands and knees, gathered up my papers and put them into large crates, piling books on top of them to hold them down. These, along with our furniture and crockery, were to be picked up at a later time and transported. I heard the front door slide open and leaned far out the window, but all I could see were the two rickshaws and their runners waiting to take us and our immediate effects away.

Setsu came rushing up the stairs, her hair wrapped in a white cotton cloth and the sleeves of her kimono tied back to free her arms for work. Behind her were three of my students, the last of whose face and torso were hidden behind an enormous vase decorated in a lovely pattern of pale-purple hydrangeas and red dragonflies with needle-thin bodies. When they were all in the room, the last boy stopped on the landing and put the vase down. It was my best pupil, Kobayashi.

"I almost fell on my backside," he said. "My father told me to give this to you."

I told Setsu to bring them tea, and we sat in the middle of the room, surrounded by crates. One of the three was Yanaka, the pupil who had mistaken Alfred Lord Tennyson for a Japanese.

"We will miss you, Hearn-*sensei*," said Kobayashi. "You gave me so much advice."

He gestured to the two boys. Yanaka put out a short-stemmed *kiseru* pipe with a bowl of blackened bronze. The other boy presented me with an *inro*—a container consisting of little stacked gold-dusted boxes decorated with a picture of an ivory centipede entwined in a coral arabesque and a mother-of-pearl mayfly under a spray of cherry blossoms.

"Tell the teacher," said Kobayashi to them in Japanese.

Yanaka sat up stiffly on his knees, speaking each English word separately and with the greatest effort.

"Thank . . . you . . . Hearn-*sensei*." He looked at his two friends for approval. Kobayashi indicated that he should continue. "I . . . am . . . sorry. Please . . . ac-cept . . . these from us. They are only . . . takens."

"Tokens," whispered Kobayashi. "To-kens."

Yanaka pronounced "tokens" quickly, as if it were a Japanese word. I smiled and thanked him. He relaxed his shoulders and neck, sighing with relief, as Setsu came into the room with hot green tea and mugwort-flavored rice cakes.

"I am sorry. We are so pressed that this is all I can offer you," she said to the boys in Japanese. The boys were too terrified with shyness to so much as look at her.

Matsue

After the better part of an hour had passed, the rickshaw, with our essential personal effects secured to the seat, was ready to go. Akira, holding Edgar so that he would not run after us, was waiting beside the other rickshaw as my wife and I, followed by my three pupils, came outside. My eye was almost blinded by the light. Kobayashi carried the large vase to the rickshaw. He tripped on a stepping stone, barely maintaining his balance. The vase jumped from his grip and appeared to stand in the air. He snapped his head toward me and flung his arms around the vase in a tight embrace. Akira went to him with arms extended, but he seemed reluctant to release it. Akira said something to him and he passed the vase carefully to him. One of the runners then took the vase from Akira and, after wrapping it in a thick woolen blanket, tied it firmly to the back of our rickshaw.

I told Setsu to climb onto the empty rickshaw, then faced Akira and the three boys. I took off my wide-brimmed hat and for some seconds bowed from the waist. When I straightened up again I saw that they were all bawling like infants.

We left them there, in front of our house, and started to climb the hill for our long journey.

Just before we arrived at the top of the hill, where we could overlook the Sea of Japan for what might be the last time, another rickshaw appeared at the top, approaching ours from the opposite direction. Riding in it were a foreign man who looked to be in his mid-twenties and a Japanese lady of somewhat riper vintage. The man wore a celluloid collar, blue glasses and a sun helmet. The woman was heavily made up with rouge on both cheeks and her chin, and a white powder caked on her neck, front and back. The man, speaking in English with an American accent, several times ordered the runner to stop. Setsu, visibly repulsed—as I had never seen her before—by the sight of her decorated compatriot, was staring at her own feet, speaking to herself in whispers.

"Excuse me, excuse me, I do beg your pardon," said the man. "May I have a word with you?"

I nodded and smiled.

"Are we in the town of Ma-tsoo-ee? I have been asking this runner and this, uh, lady beside me time and time again, but their babbling hardly makes civilized sense."

"I see. Yes, the town is just down this hill and off to the left."

"Thank you, sir, I am very grateful to you. Oh, and one more thing, please. May I?"

"By all means."

"Do you know in town where I might find Mr. Lafcadio Hearn, the author? I understand that he is there."

Setsu, who did not speak more than a few dozen words of English, threw me a sharp sidelong glance.

"Never heard of him," I said. "I do not live in Matsue."

"Oh, I see. Sorry to have troubled you. Please accept this in return. Pectopah's the name, with the stress on the 'pah.' It is a Russian surname. I am the progeny of Russians, oh, some generations back now, I am afraid to say."

He stood up in his rickshaw, reached out and handed me a book.

"Thank you."

"The pleasure has been mine, sir, I assure you. Now, if I may intrude on your time just once more, would you please tell this man to take us down the hill, and not so chop-chop as before? I may be a globetrotter, but I am not accustomed to rickshaw runners who act like daredevil French balloonists."

The American man chuckled at his timely little simile, poking his index finger into the side of his lady friend, who had been fixing her gaze ahead during our conversation. She covered her mouth, giggled and pulled his finger away from her side. I instructed the runner to take the two of them to Matsue, without mentioning pace. He grunted and immediately picked up his

Matsue

poles, jerked the rickshaw forward and began to run quickly down the hill. The jerk sent Mr. Pectopah springing back into his seat.

The runner of our rickshaw took us to the top of the hill, followed closely by the rickshaw with our goods. I felt around the back and patted the blanket protecting my large vase.

From the top of the hill the sea looked strikingly blue, with not a cloud in the sky to smear the tone. I brought the book in my hand close to my face and ran my eye over its cover: *Amorous Adventures in Forbidden Zones* by Walter G. Pectopah. I waited until we were moving at a steady pace along the flat road at the foot of the hill before tossing the book away. I aimed my toss. I didn't want it to land in the paddies that lined the road. I was delighted that it ended up in a ditch overgrown with tall yellowish weeds.

I could not see Setsu's face. She was sitting on my blind side. But I sensed that she was smiling to herself. At least I think it was to herself.

1894–1895   Kobe

I was feeling more and more Japanese. During my stay in Kumamoto I had often been taunted by rowdy boys and little thugs, both calling me *ijin*, or foreigner, the former in loud nervous screams and the latter softly, spasmodically, embarrassingly under the breath. I certainly did not mind these attacks. The Japanese had long been victims of unjust treatment at the hands of Europeans and Americans, being forced to do this or that, sacrificing all profit, both material and spiritual, in the wicked bargain. A few epithets flung at the white man on the street hardly constituted a crime. When the boys threw stones, I picked them up and pretended to munch on them.

But in Kobe, even shortly after my arrival, I had become upset by the street urchins pointing me out with jeering and sneers. I knew that they were aiming not at me but at other foreigners—the base, ludicrous, offensive and pompous white-skinned residents of the port town. If anything I wanted to join the harassing chorus.

I was invited to one of their presumably exclusive white man's clubs, exclusive if for nothing else than explicit policy: NO JAPANESE OR WOMEN ALLOWED. I reluctantly took up the invitation at the misguided urging of my curiosity. I found these members and their guests to be a group dining out on ignorance and feigning a façade of superiority. They despised the Japanese yet each one had his own precious "little friend," usually a servant, gardener or rickshaw runner. Such informants were, I was assured, the salt of the earth and the source of their own sworn devotion to everything quaintly Oriental. All the while these Europeans and Americans relegated their Japanese counterparts—people of their own station and intelligence—to a heap of loathing. Any sincere effort to effect equality on the part of those Japanese was seen as pretense, any attempt at congruent communication as presumptuousness. So naturally I took to wearing Japanese clothes in Kobe. I felt more myself in them.

The war in China did not end until April of my second year in Kobe, 1895, causing much worry in the foreign "community." While, on the one hand, some, particularly the English, were happy to see one yellow race thinning out the ranks of another— a "sorely needed tonsure," as one foreigner put it, "for the Oriental races"—the very thought that the Japanese might be victorious and begin to raise their head and shoulders to the level of Occidental ones disturbed and infuriated them. Japan would probably, I had predicted, control China. The only road to its own independence from Occidental bullies lay in outside conquest.

Yet with all of the problems caused by such international commotion, I myself was considerably more agitated by what was happening in the mind of the Japanese, by the loss of the old values, the humble courtesies, the sweet inconsistencies, that which Occidentals took to be contradictions and hypocrisies but which I knew to be the essence of the true innocent spirit of the people. If I could redress that loss by but a single decimalized digit, my mission, I knew, would someday be recognized.

I felt safer in Kobe than in Kumamoto. Earthquakes were rarer, for one thing. I had detested nights in Kumamoto spent in the bamboo grove waiting for tremors to subside. We who were not born here cannot live normally in the presence of constant disaster. I admire the Japanese for their ability to put it out of their minds. It is the touchstone of their resignation. If one can be calm in the face of this infernal quaking, then one can learn Japanese toleration of anything. I, for one, did not have it. Where

Kobe

the Japanese waved off coincidental misfortune, I grumbled and protested. When they smiled and ignored stupidity or sin in others, I lashed out and trembled.

My desk at the *Kobe Chronicle*, where I was hired to write editorials and articles of local interest, was in a similar state of disarray as my table, now no longer my valise, at home. Disorder for the person who creates it has its own logic. The do-gooder who comes along and "rationalizes" the space only makes its inhabitant lose his peace. I did reserve, however, a neatly cleared area on the desk for my *kiseru* pipes, my gold-dusted *inro* in which I kept my shag tobacco, my humidor for my cigars, my tiny-drawered paulownia-wood desk cabinet where I stored my cigarette papers, and my large chipped-glass ashtray which held my Turkish meerschaum. Smoking, unlike writing, requires etiquette.

There were five other people with desks in the room, all Japanese except for one, an American named Jim who read galley proofs. I never bothered to ask his last name. With Americans one established an immediate intimacy and used the first name as if to prove it. It was only after a long acquaintanceship that one realized this intimacy to be a veneer, that it took only a single word of grating opinion to set one against his grain. The American variety of informality was rigid and constraining, its purpose to keep people ignorant of—and thereby civil toward—each other. I much preferred people who kept their distance until such time as a confluence of view and disposition suggested an appropriate approach.

My desk stood flush against a wall under a large window. I could observe people on the streets. How different this was from every other picture I had had of Japan, how much more like—or trying to be like—what I had witnessed in Dublin, London, New York, Cincinnati, New Orleans or Philadelphia. Those pictures for me were part of another life—my non-Japanese life—clouded pictures, dim, fading and unrecognizable. Perhaps in time those images will vanish altogether, leaving only matte.

I was called out of the office to the police headquarters. These were located in a two-story brick building. My runner left me off in front of it. I was met at the door and taken to the basement, where an enormous iron door was unlocked and opened for me. In the room stood a dozen large tables, and on the tables lay naked corpses. Two of them were of infants. They looked like ceramic dolls, their legs up in the air as if kicking, their mouths open fully. Two policemen pointed simultaneously to a table in the corner. On it lay the corpse of a Japanese man. He appeared to be in his late twenties. He was lying flat on his back with both hands by his sides, a small white flaxen cloth covering the genitals.

I was transported back to the morgues in Cincinnati and New Orleans, where I had spent many a happy hour examining the black, white and brown corpses and chatting amiably with the dissectors. The atmosphere there had banished my shyness and I was able to release a quality inside myself that rendered distrust wholly unnecessary. I once stayed overnight at the morgue and never remembered waking up so refreshed—a new man. This inner freedom was, however, restricted to contact with the deceased.

The policemen and I were joined by another Japanese. He introduced himself as Goro Izumi, a newspaper reporter with the popular daily, the *Yorozu Choho*. I introduced myself, and he said, "Yes, I have heard much about you, Mr. Hearn."

"Are you here to look at this man?" I asked him.

"No. I am here to look at you," he replied.

I found this reply puzzling and wondered if I had properly understood his intent. My more than four years in Japan had given me a profound insight into the soul of the Japanese but not much more than a widely spread smattering of familiarity with the colloquial sense of irony.

I took my magnifying glass from my vest pocket and conducted a thorough examination of the skin as I had been taught by my dissecting comrades in Cincinnati and New Orleans. There were no marks from puncture wounds. The redness about the neck

Kobe

indicated that the man, in all probability, had died from hanging. I asked if I might have the body turned over. The two policemen obliged.

"Have you found what you came for, Mr. Hearn?"

I smiled at the Japanese reporter, nodding that I had. This corpse was sturdily built, strikingly handsome, and tall for a Japanese.

Some thirty minutes later Goro Izumi and I were sitting on a bench overlooking the harbor. Japanese laborers were rushing about below like dervishes, unloading immense bundles of cargo from two foreign vessels.

"It was no coincidence that I came to the police headquarters when you were present, Mr. Hearn," said Goro Izumi in perfectly accented American English. "I had been hoping to meet you for some time."

"Well, you encountered me at the right place."

"I think so," he said, grinning.

"You see, what others find repugnant, I am attracted to. What others find macabre, I deem to be exquisite and beautiful."

"Yes, I have read your writing. It so happens that I was a student in Boston when your essays about the town of Matsue were published in *Harper's Magazine*. I am more interested in your ideas about Japan than I am in anybody else's."

"You flatter me, Mr. Izumi."

"Please call me Goro. I am used to it from my Boston days."

"Very well."

We sat in silence for some moments.

"You see," I said, "I was terribly shy as a reporter in Cincinnati and New Orleans, much too shy, actually, to practice my profession properly. I was known to pace for hours outside the house of a man I was sent to interview. I could not bring myself to knock on his door and face him. But when it came to corpses I could go right up to them. One thing about corpses, Goro, they permit one's natural curiosity to conquer one's apprehension."

"Mr. Hearn," he said, abruptly standing. "May I invite you to have a cup of coffee with me? Can you spare me the time for this?"

"I suppose that I can," I said, knocking the ash from the bowl of my meerschaum on the edge of the bench.

He took me to an Occidental-style coffee house not far from the offices of the *Kobe Chronicle*. I offered him a cigar, but he refused. I lit one for myself and stared at him, one eye through thick smoke.

"Mr. Hearn," he said. "Please forgive my directness. I do not mean to be rude to such an eminent author and genuine advocate of Japanese life as you."

"Not at all. I do not know what you mean. And as for being an expert, perhaps I merely appear to be such by wearing this kimono and these *tabi* socks. I assure you, I do it to be comfortable and to distinguish myself from the puffed and self-propelling rabble of Occidentals that one tries so hard to avoid in this town."

"I understand. At least I think I do. You see, I avoided other Japanese in Boston like the plague. Anyway, well, oh, why don't you wear glasses, Mr. Hearn? Please forgive me."

I laughed heartily, choking momentarily on my own cigar smoke.

"Oh, is that what you wanted to know? A most logical question. The reason is simple. I once caught dengue fever in New Orleans and was so low on money after recovering that I was forced to pawn my glasses. I haven't worn any since. They might still be in the pawnshop if I went back to claim them."

He was writing something down in a small notebook as we were brought two coffees by a waitress dressed as a housemaid. The coffee was served in large bowls, as if it were ceremonial tea.

Kobe

Perhaps someday the Japanese would so master Occidental custom, I thought, that they would transform their tea ceremony into a coffee ceremony with the great master grinding the beans as his disciples listened reverently to the soft crushing of grounds and the honored guests sipped the bitter liquid from armchairs upholstered in gold and silver silk brocade. Yes, it was bound to happen. At such a time in the future readers could recall Japan now as a mere dream, the dream of Lafcadio Hearn.

"Are you doing an interview with me? If so, I should sit up straight. I must not slouch when pontificating about Japan."

"Oh, Mr. Hearn, I am decidedly one who appreciates your ironical wit. Our readers are fascinated by visitors from abroad, by what they have to say about Japan."

"I would rather not be included in that mob."

"Oh, I am sorry. I understand. When I was in Boston I was most ashamed of my countrymen who were there. They were petty and miserly, and they acted like crude little shaven monkeys toward the tall, proud Americans. What our readers want to know is what you will be writing about Japan in the future."

"More books. Books about the heart, Goro, the *kokoro* of Japan. I see it so clearly. As for my opinions on the foreigners who have come here to live off the Japanese and the missionaries who are here to suck out their souls, I will continue to write about those transient phenomena in my editorials. Just yesterday I spoke with an American missionary. He was proud of the fact that he had dragged a ninety-two-year-old woman away from her deathbed to set fire to her Buddhist altar. The woman died shortly after that, but the missionary was satisfied that she would now find her place in heaven. I told the missionary that the very same fire that transported her to his heaven would be the one which would burn a hundred times more brightly in his own personal hell."

Goro was writing this down. The long ash from my cigar dropped into the ashtray, and I looked around the room. There were some two dozen Japanese there, but I was the only one dressed in kimono.

"Very interesting, Mr. Hearn. Thank you very much."

"If you would like to hear something much more interesting and, perhaps, shocking to your readers, Goro, I will tell you."

"Oh yes, please. As you know better than anyone, readers are drawn to the shocking."

"I am not Lafcadio Hearn."

"I beg your pardon?"

"No. You heard me correctly. I am not Lafcadio Hearn."

"I do not understand. There are many foreign gentlemen in Kobe, but none who resembles you, Mr. Hearn. There are some things that no man can escape from."

"Foreign gentlemen? I do not know whether to take that as a compliment on your part or a serious flaw in your reportorial judgment. Be that as it may, my name is no longer Lafcadio Hearn."

Goro was looking at me with his mouth agape.

"I have recently become a Japanese citizen, having been adopted legally into my wife's family. My surname is Koizumi. My given name is Yakumo, which means 'the myriad clouds' and is also a poetic equivalent of Izumo, the old provincial name."

"Yakumo . . . Koizumi."

"Correct. Oh, do not let your coffee get cold, Goro."

He picked up his bowl without taking his eyes off me.

"Had I remained a British subject, my wife would not have been able to inherit my property. Now that I am a Japanese, she will be able to do so."

"I find it strange to hear Lafca . . . I mean, Yakumo Koizumi referring to his property. Does this mean that you are denouncing your ideals? Now that you are becoming Japanese, you are turning out to be materialistic like all of the rest of us."

"Is that a question?"

"Uh, yes. I am sorry."

"Not at all. I must look after the poor little woman. You see, I once thought that staying too long in any one place was sufficient to destroy all one's illusions about it. This is true, actually, particularly of a place such as the United States. The only way to retain one's illusions about that country is to focus them entirely on straightforward material betterment. Japan, on the other hand, has chaos at its core. The closer one approaches that core, the deeper one fathoms the world of illusion and warped contradiction. Such a country is begging for citizens such as Yakumo Koizumi, that is, me."

He asked if he could tell his readers that I had become a Japanese, adding that this would be a "scoop," a word I was not familiar with.

"Certainly," I said. "Only native-born Japanese hide the things that are most important to them. You see how Japanese I am? I am already deriding my own people."

We stood outside the coffeehouse, about to part.

"A man's profession is more crucial to him than his nationality, Goro. We newspaper writers have one thing in common, no matter what country we decide to be ours, and that is our allegiance to our readers. Who knows? You might have easily become an American and changed your name too. Perhaps you will someday, if you believe that this will bring you closer to your readers."

"I did consider it once."

"Well, there you are. Now take a suicide, one of the most tragic incidents for us to deal with. The concern of the reporter, Goro, should always be primarily with the weapon. It is details that conjure reality. He shot himself with a fine English Tranter worth at least seventy-five dollars. Or, he placed the small silver-mounted Smith & Wesson to his right temple and . . . You see, it is not the temple itself that is important, it is the fact that it was the right one. It is not the method he chose to dispose of himself; it is the fact that the weapon was a Smith & Wesson and that it was silver mounted. Japanese newspapers are in their infancy, as you know. If I can teach you one thing, it is how to reconstruct reality."

I walked back to the newspaper offices alone. It was early evening. Young men were practicing military marches on the streets. Japanese flags flew from virtually every building and house. In the front hall of our offices I picked up a copy of the evening edition of the newspaper. The headlines read, "Major Victory for Japanese Troops in China. Over 3,000 Russians Killed at Port Arthur."

I retied the thin obi around my waist and went outside again. I wanted to write the article about the corpse I had examined. I was thinking about Goro. In some ways he reminded me of Akira Hosoi in Matsue. But the two young men were dissimilar in the fundamental nature of their Japaneseness, Akira's being rooted in the land's subsoil. Goro was worldlier and, I daresay, open-minded. But these were the very qualities that were causing Japan to err in blind imitation of the Occident. Japanese were at their ugliest when they tried to be like someone else.

My eyesight was deteriorating, and I was forced to leave the employ of the *Kobe Chronicle*. No matter how dearly I cherished the notion, shared by Setsu, of returning to live in Matsue, I had no doubt but that the climate there would take my sight away from me forever. The tropics would have been ideal, but the devil knew when I would be able to extricate myself from Japan and my obligations to family here. During the winter in Kobe a severe fever caused my eyesight to fail, and neuritis threatened retinal detachment. My oculist, a kind German resident—the non-British, non-American foreign inhabitants of this town were, on oc-

Kobe

casion, tolerable—ordered me to sit in darkness for three weeks. I naturally complied. The total blackness freed my imagination, bringing it that much nearer to precision.

It was the end of the winter of 1895. Little Setsu was not so little. She was eight months pregnant—by Occidental reckoning, that is. The Japanese calculated the months of pregnancy in another way, considering the full term to be not nine, but ten months. Setsu was thus nine months pregnant. I supposed that this was similar to the way the British and the Americans reckoned their stories, the former calling the floor on the ground level as "ground," the latter calling it the "first." It did not change which floor one was on.

The ages of people were reckoned differently as well. A child was one year old when born then became two at the New Year. I found both of these measurements most satisfactory. That which defied the false universality of logic was, by definition in my book, satisfactory.

I normally arrived home from the newspaper offices at six o'clock and was met in the entryway by Setsu, who took my briefcase and coat. I would trudge upstairs, undressing and discarding the garments as I climbed, and put on my house kimono which was left, folded neatly, for me on the *zabuton* cushion. On warmer days I sat for some time in my undergarments and called downstairs, "Beer." One might say, cynically, that I had become a dyed-in-the-wool Japanese. But I had acted like this all my adult life. There are some traits for which the Japanese claim of uniqueness is specious.

At 11:30 on an early March night, I held in my hand the evening edition of the *Kobe Chronicle*, which carried what was destined to be a controversial article. The article read as follows:

Japan is breaking down the immense power of China, creating a new Korea by enlarging her territory, and, by doing so, altering the entire political face of the East forever.

Roger Pulvers

> Ever since American ships forced Japan out of its state of national isolation in the 1850s, she has been a land of fears and doubts. Her people have been treated, both as nationals and as individuals, with, at best, a twittering condescension. This condescension, alas, remains and will probably be an everlasting feature of the puffed Occidental mind.
> But the fears and doubts are, thankfully, disappearing from the chambers of the Japanese mind, and Japan can—and will!—join the world's powers on an equal footing.

The article was signed "Y. K." I put the newspaper over my chest, laying it out like a little blanket, and on top of that I placed a copy of my latest book published in the United States. Its title and my name appeared on the cover: *Out of the East* By Lafcadio Hearn.

I fell asleep with my two pieces of writing in my two names over my chest and my head propped up on my wooden pillow. They say that a man who sleeps with a "tall pillow" sleeps without worry. I did not dream that night, or if I did, I did not recall doing so.

I had spent my life until then wishing that I could go to other places, craving other smells and desiring to be away from people who had come to know me. But on that late winter night those wishes, cravings and desires had left me. There was no trace of them in any thought or feeling. I was content to be at my home, Japan, and it was, precisely, the Japan which I had created that was providing the contentment.

Lafcadio Hearn had given life to Yakumo Koizumi and was now about to live it to full advantage.

The cherry blossoms were in full bloom when Goro Izumi and I visited a local shrine at festival time. Once these odorless flowers blossomed I was not interested in them. I much preferred the buds. The promise of the flower is intriguing, the flower itself a blatant and tedious symbol.

Kobe

Cherry blossoms that appeared at odd times, however, as if in defiance of the season, pleased me no end. I was drawn to things out of their place, and a little pink blossom in the autumn, known in Japan as *kuruizaki*, or insane blooming, was an invention of gods who cherish the muses doing their bidding.

The Japanese festivalgoers were reveling in their sky of pink petals, though they were, in every manner of appearance, a contrast to those pilgrims and carousers whom I had seen in Matsue some five years earlier. This was to be expected in a bustling town of over two hundred thousand inhabitants, five times more numerous than in my lovely and somber village on the Sea of Japan.

There was yet another contrast. Nearly all of the games, toys and amusements of the Kobe shrine festival were oriented to war. We passed by one man selling a toy made of skillfully carved and twisted bamboo. It depicted a Japanese soldier beheading a Chinese coolie. The man pulled a lever and the soldier's tiny shining sword swung down. When it struck the coolie's neck, the head, with coolie hat attached, lopped off, rolled down an oiled chute and landed in a small basket, to the squealing delight of the boys in attendance.

One boy begged his father to buy the toy for him. As the father was asking the price, we walked away. There were also old samurai swords and armor for sale, with very few apparent takers. A man, oblivious to the fact that only hoarse snippets of his patter were heard by passersby, was shouting out the passages of a story about a brave samurai during the *Sengoku Jidai*, the period of the warring provinces some four centuries in the past. Colored woodblock prints on a table beside him, most of them crudely finished, portrayed scenes of Chinese battlegrounds, all of them heroic poses of Japanese victory. Two soldiers passed us by, applauded by a small group of country people who had opened stalls to sell vegetables, such as the large white *daikon* Chinese radish, Japanese *myoga* ginger and shiitake mushrooms.

"I am sorry for this," said Goro.

"Why? What do you mean?"

"These people are so vulgar."

"Vulgar? Not any more than all people are vulgar. 'Vulgar' means common, remember, as all humans are common in their bones."

"But all they value is victory. It does not matter to them what brutality is committed to achieve it."

"Then that makes them all the more like others," I said. "Why should Japan alone be made to feel uneasy about being a strong nation?"

"You saw those colored prints. It is as if only the Japanese are heroes in the world. Everyone else must bow down to Japan."

"No European power was ever embarrassed by its conquests, Goro."

"But Russia, Germany and France are not happy with Japan. They see us as a threat to the world."

"Who cares about Russia, Germany and France, eh? Do you know why they are not happy, as you say? Because Japan's gains in China are their losses. Sour grapes from sour vines, my friend. The Chinese had European guns helping them. If they hadn't, Japan would have won even sooner. The Japanese navy was far from strong, but it crushed the Chinese fleet in two engagements nonetheless, without the loss of a single vessel."

Goro gave me a puzzled look. But surely he had read the newspapers and knew the facts of the matter.

"These victories, as you call them, Mr. Koizumi, only feed the Japanese pride. I am afraid of my people when they get too much pride in them. There is nothing wrong with a nation that is satisfied. But we Japanese are dangerous when we move ahead fast. We are unable to be equal with others. We require that they be our angels or our slaves. We envisage them as such and force them

Kobe

to act like that. Those who do not, we ignore, reject or eliminate. Look what we have done to the foreigners lately."

"What have you done?"

"Foreigners now have to pay a special high price for everything: haircuts, theater tickets, lodgings, even a cup of tea."

"They have more money, so why shouldn't they pay? Up until now they have had all of the privileges under the sun. Do not chastise the Japanese for trying to redress an unequal balance."

We had been strolling along as we talked. We came to a stop in front of a somewhat inebriated man who was recounting an experience to a dozen or so young men in student uniform.

"I was at the battle," he was saying, "so I can tell it to you straight from the horse's mouth. Ganjiro, yeah, that was his name, 'cause, though, uh, some men called him Genjiro. But he . . . anyway, he was our burglar. No wait. I mean, bugler, the, he was, of our regiment, and the best damn, uh, so, bugler in the mikado's army. Well, he was blowin' his bugle, for us to assemble or somethin', I don't quite remember the details, 'cause, but I was there, right there, standin' next to him, Genjiro, or, so, and a damn bullet comes whizzin' along, just missed me here, right here on my left ear and hit him right above the belly, comin' out his back, shoo! Damn bullet. Went through his heart. So anyway, he falls to his knees and dies on the spot, right beside me, but you know what? He wouldn't let go of that bugle, though he was dead. His hand was wound around it with the grip of a snake, of, of Benkei on his halberd. Uh-huh. And you know what?" The man paused, reached down to a large glass filled with milky saké and took a long drink. "You know what? That bugle continued to play on, even after, uh, so, Ganjiro was dead as a stone. It played on and on like that until all us men were assembled. That was the force of his will. I was right there, I tell ya. That is the will, my boys, of the Japanese fighting man!"

He emptied his glass then nodded his head up and down several times. The students dispersed, visibly impressed with the story.

"That is my country," said Goro. "An orchestra of the dead. That is the difference between your country and mine—or should I say your former country and your new, adopted one. Your former country and those in Europe like it have true leaders. In my country the buglers are the leaders, and all others follow their lead without a thought in their heads—a procession of empty-minded fanatics following in the footsteps of dead buglers."

While Goro was unusual in Japan for his ability to examine, with some objectivity, the motivations of his people, he shared completely one of their least desirable traits: an obsequious and excessive respect for the modern vulgar Caucasian. And what did he mean by "your former country and your new, adopted one?" Was he confused as to where I had consciously chosen to place myself? Most men could never know the luxury of the imagination's rebirth. I had only one country: my Japan.

There was no time, unfortunately, to explain these things to Goro, for we ran into Jim, who informed me of a grave turn of events. I immediately left the two of them at the shrine and rushed out, bumping into a soldier by the gate and removing my hat as he cursed me. I had to lift the hem of my kimono to dash through the streets without stumbling.

I arrived at a small wooden house located at the address Jim had given me. The front door was open, but I waited to enter until I could catch my breath. It was a very shabby home in a poor area of the city. A Japanese police detective came out of the doorway, recognizing me.

"Ah, Mr. Hearn. So you came after all," he said.

"May I go in?"

"Yes. You are authorized."

Kobe

It was dark in the dirt-floor entryway. I removed my shoes and stepped up into the house. My eye was still unused to the dark. I stood still for a moment, taking deep breaths. Another policeman came from the inner room.

"Are you the newspaperman?" he asked.

"Yes, that is correct."

"*A, so* . . . I see," he said, looking my Japanese attire up and down.

There was an unpleasant tone of mockery in this most neutral of Japanese expressions, "*A, so.*"

"Follow me."

I went with him into the inner room, which had a single lantern hanging on twine from the ceiling. The whole house was made of the flimsiest wood as if it were but an enlarged matchbox. Were an earthquake to strike at that instant, I thought, we would all be knocked flat as if inside a house of cards.

On the floor in the middle of the room lay the dead body of a young blond Caucasian woman.

"Hanged herself," said the policeman.

A small patch of dried blood had formed at the base of her nose. I stood over her, suddenly teetering and feeling faint. The policeman grabbed me firmly by the arm.

"I thought that you should see this," said the policeman, "seeing as she is an American like you."

It would be no use telling him then that I was not—indeed had never been—an American.

"Who is she?" I asked.

"The wife of the Japanese man who committed suicide," said the detective from before, coming into the room. "You came to examine his body some time ago. Do you remember? It was at police headquarters. Now his wife has followed him into the other world. Pity. She's quite beautiful."

The policeman was still holding my arm. I was grateful for this.

"Uh, I . . . yes, I do remember."

"Perhaps you should have this, as a sort of souvenir. I can't read this sideways language of yours. It's your newspaper, isn't it? The dead woman was clutching it when she died."

He handed me a copy of the *Kobe Chronicle*, the edition carrying my article on her husband's death with the details of the condition in which I had found his corpse.

"A neighbor told us that she had been very upset by an article in your newspaper, about how her husband put an end to his life and what his body looked like after he died. I don't know. None of us can read that. And I don't suppose the neighbors can either. You'll have to judge for yourself, Mr. Hearn."

I extricated my arm from the policeman's grip and stared at the detective, my eye clouding over. I blinked over and over again, but the semi-opaque white film would not vanish.

"I suppose you will want to examine this body with your magnifying glass," he said. "I think that under the circumstances, however, we shall have to deny you that privilege, even though you are a respected foreigner and of the same race as the *hotokesan*."

He had used the Japanese word for "departed soul" or "corpse" that literally meant "Buddha." I walked out of the house in a daze, leaving my shoes in the entryway. The policeman came running after me, carrying them. He apologized to me as he handed them to me. It was the first sunny day of spring, with no breeze to blow even the barest few cherry blossom petals off their branches. I took my hat off and placed my shoes in it, walking like that, barefoot and bareheaded, in the direction of my home.

Kobe

I was smoking my precious *gankubi* "gooseneck" *kiseru* pipe, with its bamboo stem more than a foot long. Jim was sitting on my desk. It was surprising that he could find the space.

"Why don't you open your eyes a bit more? Oh, no offense intended, Mr. Hearn," he said. "I meant it only as a figure of speech."

"No offense taken, Jim. After all, I live in a perpetual cloud, don't I? Only figuratively, as you say."

Jim coughed and picked up a sheaf of my notes, putting them down immediately.

"What I mean to say is the emperor has issued an edict that one-tenth of all government salaries will have to now go for purchases of warships, no ifs, ands or buts about it. And if that isn't enough, he has designated hundreds of new nobles: dukes, marquises, counts—I dunno how to pronounce it—viscounts, or whatever you call 'em, and barons. We're gonna have to be darn careful now when we call people things. Have to get their highfalutin' handles right. Jesus, the Japanese are bad enough when the war's on, but they're even worse when it's over."

"Uh-huh."

I relit my pipe and focused my eye on the page of an open book.

"Is that all you can say, 'uh-huh'?"

"What else is there to say?"

"Well, at least you could have an opinion. Every man has to have an opinion. If he doesn't, he's not participatin' in a real way in freedom and somebody's gotta give him an opinion, even if it has to be, you know, encouraged on him."

"Encouraged on him? Is that the American way?"

"Look, Mr. Hearn. I don't know much about you, but I do know that you got a whole lot of benefits out of living in the United States of America. Nobody's gonna take your opinion away from you. God knows you're entitled to it so long as it doesn't run roughshod over the opinions of the rest of us. But remember, you are from the old world, just like these Japanese. You got all those titles an' things too, where you come from, England or somethin'. We got rid of that in our revolution with you redcoats, an' now we got freedom. If the Japanese want freedom they're gonna have to pick themselves up from where they are and get rid of all this pent-up aggressiveness. They've taken Formosa, and they dominate Korea. It's only a matter of time before they take on Russia; everybody knows that. They're gonna have an empire. You wait an' see."

"What strong country doesn't have one?"

"Mine. Mine doesn't. That's why we fight, to wrest control of far-flung places out of the hands of imperialists."

I could not keep from bursting into laughter. For some reason this caused Jim to cough several times, rather vehemently, and I didn't have the heart to ask him what his country planned to do with those "far-flung places" once control was wrested from others.

"I can see you're laughing at me, and, frankly, I don't get your sense of humor, Mr. Hearn," he said. "Where would Japan be without the United States, eh? A little dark yella island of people shut up in a little dark yella hole, that's where."

"Please, Jim, just one favor, if you will. Do not call me Mr. Hearn. My name is Mr. Koizumi. You can pronounce that. Or, well, you Americans use first names all the time, don't you? When you pat someone on the back, eh? Call me Ya-ku-mo. Okay, Jim?"

Jim stood, waving away the smoke from my pipe with both his hands.

"You don't belong anywhere, Mr. Hearn. You lived off the best hospitality of us Americans and now you're living off the Japanese. You oughta remember one thing. Nobody—and I mean

Kobe

nobody, least of all Japanese people—likes a man who doesn't belong anywhere."

He started to walk out of the room. The Japanese at their desks had made not the slightest sign that they were listening to our conversation.

"One more thing you ought not to forget, Mr. Hearn," he said, turning in the doorway. "And sorry, I cannot pronounce your new name. It was us who gave them everything they got: architecture, mail, the telegraph, railroads, better mining, prison reform—though I don't really know about that myself—sanitation reform, medical reform, cotton and paper mills just like we got, waterworks—even their harbors come from us. And now they turn on us. Us, Mr. Hearn. That includes you too. You may not want to see yourself that way, but they sure will. You can bet your bottom dollar on that, sir."

Jim walked out. I looked at the Japanese in the room one by one. They had their heads lowered and were staring, without blinking, at the tops of their desks. The tobacco in my pipe had turned to ash. Without emptying it, I put a pinch of fresh tobacco in the bowl and tamped it down with the tip of my baby finger. The char inside had become so thick that my baby finger was the only one that fit. I struck a match and gazed out the window. It was an early evening in mid-April. I could see, in absolutely exquisite detail encompassing everything at once in my eye's range, scores of men, many of them walking swiftly, as if with a unique purpose in mind. The manner of their dress, their gait, their every gesture and bodily expression were clear to me. But I could see no women on this street. It was as if all Japan consisted of men, and this precise time in the evening, here and now, was the only moment that seemed to count.

How did I remember her whereabouts? The route escapes me now. No amount of concentration can bring back those things which, for reasons unknown to us, we block from our minds.

Whatever led up to the event is lost. Perhaps this loss is entwined in the portent of the event itself.

I detested trains and made a point to avoid them at all costs. Yet I found myself on one, traveling from Kobe to Osaka. The Kobe foreigners delighted in referring to Osaka as "that crass commercial center," not realizing that all commerce is crass and the exploitative variety of it in which they themselves were so wholeheartedly engaged as middlemen, the most socially unredeemable and putrid form of all.

I rode third class, as had been my custom in my scavenging days in London. The train car was as filthy as a New Orleans opium den, and even more crowded. Women bore on their backs enormous square loads wrapped in blue *furoshiki* cloths without stitching. From their odor, which reached me across the wagon, these were no doubt Chinese radishes pickled in rice bran. Some of these women, among them very old ones with backs bent like a set square, were obliged to stand. No man of any age, neither the little boys with dirt-caked faces and runny noses nor the men sitting cross-legged on the benches eating rice dumplings and drinking cold saké, stood to offer a seat. There were a few disabled soldiers, one of them with no legs at all, propped up on the bench like a ventriloquist's dummy, picking his teeth with a long metal skewer, while a man who looked to be in his eighties was holding his wooden false teeth proudly on his open palm, removing bits of food with the sharpened nail of his fourth finger. The old man nonchalantly swung his head to one side and spit a generous glob of sputum into the aisle, where it fell amid cigarette butts, a few toppled beer bottles that rolled back and forth with the movement of the train, spilled tea and other rubbish of a nondescript nature. None of this bothered me in the least, and I certainly saw no contradiction between it and the demonic aesthetic refinements so recently associated around the world with the word "Japanese."

The train passed through a factory district, its black smoke billowing and mingling with that produced by hundreds of small wooden shacks. In the open doors of some of these shack-factories, men stripped to their loincloths were working with an admirable speed and diligence. No one in the train bothered to look at them except me.

Some time later, I was walking along an unpaved side road in Osaka, in a district that the British would call the "back slums." I passed a ramshackle building with a woman in ragged Occidental dress standing outside. Above the building's door was a red sign in peeling paint that read "GLAND HOTEL."

I soon arrived at a nearby two-story house after asking an old woman in the area the way. The house itself was an old one, but, judging from the sheen of the paint, the front window had obviously recently been covered with narrow crimson slats. I knocked twice on the front door and entered. The darkness inside was nearly total, and my eye could discern only the vague outline of a figure halfway along the hall.

"What do you want?" said the figure, a woman's.

"Um, excuse me. I am sorry, but I am looking for a woman."

"Nothing to be sorry about. If you had eyes you'd see some in front of you."

With my eye slightly more accustomed to the darkness I could see that there were five or six women sitting in a circle in a small tatami-mat room near the entryway.

"Um, no, I am sorry," I repeated. "I am looking for a particular woman."

The figure's face gradually appeared in ever-increasing gray detail before me—a middle-aged and heavily made-up woman. She led me up a flight of stairs and along a hallway. She opened a door, releasing a rush of horribly foul air.

"In there," she said. "And stop wincing."

In the room there were about two dozen young girls, all fast asleep, their rounded sides neatly pushed against each other like birds in a poulterer's window. I gave the woman what must have seemed a helpless look, taking from my pocket a one-yen note and handing it to her.

"All right, just a minute. Stay here," she said, entering the room.

I watched as she stepped effortlessly over the girls. She crouched in a corner, shaking the shoulders of one of them. The girl woke up abruptly and turned her face toward me. It was, without a doubt, Yone, Akira's little sister. She must have been twenty by then, but she looked much older. I squinted to see her more clearly and moved to one side in the doorway. The only light in the room came from the hallway.

I took Yone away from the house. Just as we reached a paved street, two soldiers in uniform turned a corner and came toward us. One of them spat at our feet. We walked without saying a word to each other. I was unable to speak. The foul odor of the room remained in my nostrils. Yone was so sickly-looking and pale that I thought that she would faint away at the first exposure to light. It was she who broke the silence in a voice barely above a whisper.

"You are very sweet," she said, smiling at me.

I was so moved by these words that I could only stare at her, my stubborn Cyclops eye awash, held tightly in its bag of hardened skin. I felt certain that this eye would burst its socket, fly off as if catapulted by rejecting muscle. My head pounded with a severe pain, causing my eye to bulge even further from its lids.

"I . . . I . . . I have . . . I am now . . . a Japanese," I finally managed to eke out.

She did not seem to understand this. Yet it did not affect the smile on her lips. I suppose that from our few encounters in Matsue, at the temple and the hospital, she had resigned herself to puzzlement over my personality. I like that about the Japanese. They never require explanations for those things which people cannot fathom. Caucasians, on the other hand, go from explanation to explanation, embracing theories until a newer one seems

Kobe

more tenable than the last. We condemn the past and are born once again into a new present, never realizing that all that went before is as much an integral part of the new self as ever. The Japanese attach trait to trait, the total always being accepted into the present.

I pulled Yone's hand sharply, and she lurched forward. This gesture alone instantly cured my headache, and I smiled back at her. I led her along the street as fast as she could go, with passersby unable to ignore us or hide their disapproving expressions. There was only one part of the city of Osaka that I knew from my studies, the place where the warehouses and wholesale dealers of cloth were located. We came to a likely building in that area, a long barrack-like structure with an elegant white facade and wide gray slats over the windows, and entered the open door.

Inside was a bustle of activity such as I had never before seen in my life in any country. Hundreds of men of all ages were engaged in inspecting, rolling and carrying bolts of cloth or simply running about. Thousands of rolls of fabric of every color imaginable were stacked along the walls of the cavernous space. Some men, no doubt the accountants and managers, sat in tatami-matted areas set off by little wooden screens. Those that I could see were rapidly fingering the beads of their abacuses. A few elegantly dressed customers sat on the edge of the raised tatami-mat floor, as one man after another brought them rolls of silk to examine.

As Yone and I entered, one of the accountants or managers hollered "Welcome, welcome" to us, prompting virtually all of the hundreds of men in the warehouse to repeat the greeting in unison. Yone flushed a bright red. I put my hand against her cheek.

I asked to be shown their most delicate and lovely fabric fit for a girl of twenty. One of the managers snapped orders in the direction of some young salesmen.

"Yes, sir, as you say, sir," replied the salesmen, again in unison, running off toward one of the walls. They returned with a single bolt of cloth. Yone watched as the cloth was unrolled before her. I did not take my eye off of her. The fabric was gold with a picture in silver and orange thread of sparrows on a twisted branch adorned in plum blossom buds.

"Do you like this one?" I asked her.

She merely nodded once, gazing off to one side, as if afraid to look me in the eye.

"I'll take this one. Have a kimono made for her and sent to her address."

"Thank you for your kindness, sir," said the manager loudly.

Hearing the words "thank you," every single man in that warehouse stopped what he was doing, turned toward Yone and me and shouted, "Thank you very much!"

After taking Yone to supper at a restaurant, I delivered her back to where she was staying. We stood at the door, once again unable to speak. She bowed to me and I bowed back.

"Oh, I forgot to ask you," I said. "How is Akira?"

Yone opened the door, speaking with her hand resting on the doorknob.

"I do not know. I do not hear from him anymore."

I stood at the closed door for some minutes, noticing for the first time that it was night. A little boy came running down the dirt road. After he had passed me, without turning around he screamed, "Foreigner! Foreigner!"

I do not recall the train trip back to Kobe nor the reason why that memory, too, has eluded me. It must be because I detest trains so thoroughly.

It was not until well past nine o'clock when I arrived home. Completely exhausted, I opened the front door without announcing myself, dropped my overcoat on the entryway floor and, my feet like lead, climbed the stairs to my study, leaning on the banister as if it were a crutch. There I shed my street clothes, donned a heavy, padded Japanese housecoat, sat at my desk, opened each of the twelve books that I was in the midst of reading to the last dog-eared page, lit my half-smoked Martinique calabash pipe from that morning and shouted "Mama-san, beer!" in the direction of the stairs.

I must have read several pages of several books before repeating my order, now in a louder voice. Setsu, I thought, must have fallen asleep, though naturally she would have done anything in her power to stay awake until her husband returned home. I put my calabash pipe and matchbox inside the large drooping sleeve of my housecoat and entered her room. She was not there. I went downstairs to the kitchen, which was spotless, if barer, than usual. As I sat at the kitchen table my hand fell upon a piece of paper. I took it to the window where the gray tumbling light from the half moon permitted me to read its message, held against my eyeball.

Byoin e mairimasu, it read in Roman letters: I am going to the hospital.

In a matter of seconds I was sprinting down the alleyway in my housecoat and wooden clogs. I could not run well in the clogs, so I kicked them off and carried them, continuing on my way in bare feet. It was a stroke of fortune that I came across a runner dozing on his rickshaw. I awakened him by shaking his shoulder vehemently. My unshaven one-eyed aquiline face but inches away from his own sent him springing from his vehicle, and, thanks to the peculiar form of humility adopted on these islands, he bowed obsequiously in apology for not being awake when I needed him.

As we raced off in the direction of the hospital, the moon was edging toward the horizon, its earthshine still distinct. I had always possessed the ability to notice in full those details which others considered extraneous. So long as they were evident at the time of a dramatic crisis, they became an integral part of—not a parenthetical addendum to—that crisis. The earthshine of the moon, disappearing as I was rushed on that particular night through the streets of the city of Kobe, was to me proof of my and my planet's existence. Ask that runner later and he could have told you that he took no such man in his rickshaw on that night, that he recalled sleeping in it himself until well past midnight. Search for the hospital and it would be there no longer, with its records destroyed and no trace to attest to its lists—births, illnesses, deaths. But the fact that I witnessed the faded light reflected from Earth onto the surface of the moon was all that I needed to verify my feelings of the moment, all that anyone needed to re-imagine the past methodically, truthfully and with a distinct clarity.

"Faster, faster," I called to the runner, who responded in the typical manner of his people to such commands by merely moving his legs more rapidly up and down without a concomitant increment in pace. In Japan, "progress"—that is, literally, moving forward—has often been the ingenious native euphemism for "running quickly in place."

I hollered and screamed at him to run faster and again faster. The poor man's legs had become pistons on a steam engine, and a virtual river of sweat poured down the shaven nape of his neck, his thin cotton coat sticking to his back, a chamois drenched in light oil. My excitement grew as we neared the hospital. Despite what I had once said, I had always wanted a child, its responses entirely unformed, a tabula rasa with no words of any race or nation written on it, a being who knew only the two poles of the magnet—laughter and weeping—with nothing yet inculcated between them to force them apart.

The runner was nearly dead from fatigue, exhaling like a smithy's bellows, his body folded in two against the side of his rickshaw.

"No money," I said, leaving my clogs on the seat. "I will pay you later."

The poor man lacked even the strength to appear humble now.

Kobe

This was my first time inside the hospital, though I knew that Setsu had come here on a number of occasions to be examined. It was a century ahead of the hospital in Matsue. Here the doctors and nurses were dressed in starched white. Two nurses, both holding corked vials of urine, marched past me, followed by a Caucasian goateed stethoscopist.

I walked down the main corridor, opening each and every door. Setsu was nowhere to be found. I soon felt a sharp tap on my shoulder and, swiveling about, saw the goateed doctor standing behind me.

"What are you looking for?" he asked in German-accented English.

"I am looking for my wife."

"What is her malady?"

"She has no malady. She is having a baby."

"Then you are in the wrong place. The maternity ward is not on the ground floor. It is up those stairs and to your right, sir."

I ran toward the stairway and up the stairs, three at a time, turned right at the top and went through a set of swinging doors. I had managed to barge in on the birth of a baby taking place at that very moment. The midwife and attending nurses were so shocked to see this panting, Occidental, whiskered ghost in their midst that they could do nothing but stare at me with mouths agape. The midwife did not release her grip on the head of the infant sticking out from the vagina of the birthing mother. Not being able to see the woman's face, for she was lying flat on her back on the wooden table, I walked around a portly red-cheeked attending nurse and took a look at the prostrate woman, my face a mere three to four inches from hers. Alas, it was not Setsu.

"*Sumimasen*," I said, "Excuse me."

I left and continued down the corridor, opening door after door and loudly calling "Mama-san, mama-san, where are you?"

into each room. The lamps had been turned off and there was no other way to find her. Finally I heard her call back to me and I knew that I had discovered the room. I went to her bed, took the matches from my housecoat sleeve and lit the kerosene lamp beside her, adjusting the flame to its lowest glow. Setsu looked up at me and smiled.

"Where is the baby?" I asked. "Boy or girl?"

"Over there. A boy," she whispered, not wanting to disturb the three other new mothers in the room, two asleep and the third nursing her newborn infant.

I went to the corner of the room where there stood three little cots with three infants wrapped in identical light brown woolen blankets, dead to the world but for the faintest short little breaths. I put my face against theirs but was unable to tell which was mine.

"Do not do that," whispered Setsu from her bed. "Do not get too close to the babies."

"But which one is mine?"

"The middle one. Everyone at the hospital says that he does not look like a Japanese."

I picked up my son. It was the first time in my life that I had had an infant in my arms, but some miraculous instinct took away my fears. I carried him to Setsu's bedside and showed him to her.

"Do you want to feed him?" I asked.

"Not now."

"Just hold him for a moment."

I passed my son to her, pulled my pipe out of my sleeve and lit it.

"Thank you," I said to her. "I'll take him back now."

His facial features had no racial significance for me. It was natural to all people around the world that a child of mixed blood resembled the other race. They only saw difference. To me this

Kobe

face had one expression only, and it lacked all reference to geography and blood, possessing, rather, the most exquisite of human expressions: blankness.

I took my son out of the room, down the stairway and along the corridor. We exited the hospital like that, just the two of us, him white and naked in his blanket, and me in my housecoat, my face a zigzag outline with its beak-like nose, globular eye and fuming pipe surrounded by stubble, barefoot, but not in the least chilled, my blood rushing inside me at what I knew to be the second triumphant time of my creative life, the first being the moment when I held my first published book in my own two hands.

It was a minute or two before I noticed that I was being followed swiftly down the street by a small crowd of doctors and nurses, including the goateed Germanic stethoscopist and the portly nurse from the birthing room. She was the spitting image of the country girls I had seen in and around Matsue some years before. The stethoscopist was flailing his arms about and shouting, "Come back here!" and "Bring that baby back this instant!" Behind him I saw the rickshaw runner. He too was waving his arms about. As he sprinted around and past the little horde of medical workers and came alongside me, I saw that he carried my two wooden clogs. The honest chap had been intent upon returning them to me, I was sure, with the thought of payment the furthest thing from his mind. With my pipe still clutched between my teeth and my son in my arms now breaking into a choking bawl, I took the clogs from him, grasping their rough twine tops through the fingers of my left hand. By now the starched parade had caught up with me and my son was whisked out of my arms by the portly nurse. Without saying a word, they all turned around and marched back into the hospital. The rickshaw runner stood beside me for a moment, as we both watched them disappear.

"I will pay you," I told him, now feeling the chill of the air and folding my arms over my chest. "I am sorry."

"Thank you, thank you, sir," he bowed apologetically. "I am terribly sorry to cause you such inconvenience."

This was known as preempting the apology of another, a clever form of Japanese one-upmanship. In the Occident your thunder is stolen. Here your rightful humility is pre-empted before you have the chance to display it.

"May I take you home, sir?" he asked.

"Yes, yes. Then I will pay you, there, at my home."

He bowed very low, and we walked together to his rickshaw. I sat on the seat as he placed a checked black-and-white travel rug over my knees. He picked up his poles and, before setting off to run, swiveled his head around to me and, opening his mouth into a bright wide and toothy smile, said, "It is a beautiful baby, sir. Looks just like a little doll."

Once home, I paid him four times the normal rate, dropped my clogs in the entryway, climbed the stairs and slipped into my futon with my housecoat on, bothering neither to drink nor eat.

I fell asleep immediately and dreamed of nothing.

The summer of that year, though stiflingly hot, saw my most productive period in Kobe. I had nearly completed another book, this one concerned primarily with Japanese religious rituals and folktale gods. I had slept through the weeks of the rainy season with a crippling fever, but thankfully it did not infect Setsu, who was nursing Kazuo, my angelic son.

One July morning I was awakened very early by the loud croaking of frogs, nature's softest and most pleasing alarm. I opened my eyes and felt myself breathing to the rhythm of the sound until my breath was broken by a shrill human bleating. Though it was not yet seven o'clock, neighbors were busy going through the excruciating motions of acquiring culture. One lady singing an aria from "La Traviata" to my left was joined in noise by someone who

Kobe

was playing a tune from Friedrich von Flotow's "Martha" to my right, a song whose false mellisonance I had been subjected to in two countries, Ireland and the United States. Now the Japanese, like the Americans, were seeing civilization as originating abroad and were founding an entire culture on copies of a distant one. If Japan continued to view its own modern enlightenment in these terms, the country it would come to resemble, the devil forbid, was sure to be the United States. As if to give credence to this early-morning theory, the individual playing "Martha" on the piano to my right, apparently a woman, started to shriek out the words to the song in English but with such a heavy accent that "Bringing in the Sheaves" came out as "Plinging in the Sheeps." Normally an accent neither amused nor offended me, but this borrowed cacophony augmented its effect and caused me to seethe.

I rushed out onto my second-story verandah, dressed as I was in absolutely nothing, and shouted to all sides at the top of my lungs.

"Shut up! All shut up!"

This brought an immediate end to the noises, and for the moment, modesty returning to me, I brought my arms to my sides and covered my genitals with crossed palms. It was then I realized that I had silenced the frogs as well.

"Oh no, not the frogs," I said, leaning over the wooden railing.

I peered down into my garden. The frogs started croaking again just as before, only now uninterrupted by the clanging and screeching of cultural pretenses designed specifically to irritate and confound the man caught in the middle. I had—if only for the time being—confounded the pretenses that surrounded me. If this was to become my only role in life, it was something I could justly be proud of.

The rhythmical frogs' sounds were broken, however, by the horn-like wail of my infant son. Setsu's head appeared from her second-story window. She glared at me.

"You woke him up," she said in Japanese, adding in English, "You shut up!" before pulling her head back inside.

I turned around and went back into my room, my face in my hands. I cherished the moments that I could find myself truly alone; even sickness was welcome if it provided me with them. They were now preciously few and far between.

It was July, and the people of Kobe were celebrating the Bon, their Festival of the Dead. Chamberlain had called it the Buddhist All Souls' Day, but I had found Chamberlain's metaphor at best distasteful, like the man himself, exuding magnanimity only to suck the resultant joy from its recipient. No Japanese custom or belief could be accurately understood in terms of Occidental comparison or term. Scholars like Basil Hall Chamberlain and all the other foreign "experts" in Tokyo were intent on nailing an ornate gilded Occidental frame around a delicately stroked Japanese picture. Despite their own pleadings of skepticism, Christ remained deeply rooted in the minds of these Caucasians, though the science of our century had proven "the savior" to be fleshless, bloodless and as vacuous as fine sand. The foreigners were never able to rid themselves of this single poisonweed burden.

In the American press I was called "an escapist." But I was no escapist—not unless I was considered to have escaped *to* something. There was no need for me to escape from a thing whose validity I had ceased to acknowledge. I faced all that I encountered headlong, never retreating, even when advised that retreat was the bland order of the moment. That was what angered my Occidental critics. Their so-called moderation marked, in reality, a total acceptance of a most barbarous Caucasian character, a sinking and wallowing, up to the small mound at the bottom of their lower lip, in excrement, all the while maintaining the pretense of "intellectual evenhandedness." I despised them all for their charitable pseudo-logic, for their sincere entertaining of both the world of decadent faith and refined argument, for their gently couched at-

Kobe

tacks on any man who wished to negate, negate and negate again the wicked white folly of Yankee-dom, Anglo-dom and the fair-haired House of Christ.

Were I to express my emotions succinctly, in the extreme terms that I felt them, could I have expected a publisher to greet me with a generous and open heart? Even a Japanese publisher would have looked politely askance, for the Japanese saw only the sweet lessons of Occidental parable, feeling profound respect for distant civilizations and harboring natural disdain for anything originating in this soil. If I was to be the despised middleman in a cynical deal—the coddled, if abandoned, interpreter between two predatory adversaries—then I would consider myself the lucky one, the sole beneficiary of all the world's doubt.

Goro Izumi appeared at the door of my study, interrupting my train of thought.

"Excuse me for startling you, Mr. Hearn," he said. "Your wife let me in."

I indicated that he should sit down. I relit my red Norwegian briar. The inside of its bowl had now become so thickly lined with carbon that a matchstick was the only object I could use to tamp tobacco into it. Soon the bowl would be entirely encrusted with the hard black substance, blocking any air through it. I had several pipes like that, and I kept them in a small rack on my desk in front of me at all times. Someday I would write, I thought, an essay about my pipes, once I figured out what, exactly, they symbolized.

"I am working on a few stories for an anthology about Japanese life," I said, "but I have become stuck at one point, Goro. May I ask you a question?"

"Of course. But I doubt whether I know anything about Japan that you have not already guessed."

"Do Japanese corpses burn blue?"

"I beg your pardon?"

I put my pipe down. No amount of inhaling or sucking could raise smoke out of it. I filled a *kiseru*, lit it, breathed a mouthful of aromatic smoke into my lungs and repeated my question.

"I do not know that," he said.

"Europeans burn blue. It is an important point. One has to get these things right, or the ghost story will lack authenticity."

"Authenticity?"

"Yes, uh, reality, correctness."

"Oh no, I know what the word means. I simply did not understand how a ghost story could have authenticity. Do you mean in the way people believe?"

"No. That is not what I mean," I said, putting my pipe down and rubbing my tearing eye.

"You are, Mr. Hearn—or Mr. Koizumi—the most inscrutable Japanese I know."

This comment caused me to laugh, and I put my hand on top of his.

"Are you still the most patriotic man in the upcoming empire?" he asked me.

"Do not patronize me, Goro. I don't mind being attacked, but I will not tolerate being patronized."

"I am not patronizing you. I know that you think we are either bowing at the feet of white men or clutching at their necks, that with us there is no in between. Yes, it is true. We are a nation of bandy-legged, ugly, nearsighted, narrow-minded grovelers."

"Then I fit in perfectly."

Now it was Goro's turn to laugh. He was a rare Japanese, a man who caught on to wit quickly.

"All we want to do," he continued, "is to stand on an equal footing with the rest of the world."

Kobe

"I know that. I have written as much time and time again, my friend. That is precisely what I am trying to urge the Japanese, my new compatriots, to do."

"Yes. But the trouble is that we may be unable to accomplish it. Your urging may have the opposite effect. It may push the Japanese too far, give them too much pride, too much of a fat spirit to go into China and prove how superior we are or how superior we think we are. When Japanese try to prove themselves, they do not know when or where to stop."

"I do marvel at your use of English, Goro. If I could speak Japanese as you speak English, I think I should become the greatest writer in the history of this country."

I took him downstairs, and we sat on the edge of the verandah, looking at the garden. I told Setsu to bring us cold barley tea and bean cakes.

"You mentioned the Japanese acting superior, or something to that effect. That is not my problem," I said.

"Isn't it?"

"To tell you the truth, Goro, I am much more concerned with two o'clock in the morning, the time when Japanese ghosts appear, than later in the morning when the ordinary man's working day begins. But you would be incorrect to think that I am oblivious to the present. I am totally immersed in it, body and soul. But, the present for me is only a convenient time to record the things which led up to it. Someday, I believe, Japan will have an empire. It is then that I shall look back, if I am alive, and judge our era now."

Goro stared out at the clump of rocks in my garden. Perhaps he had not grasped what I had, or perhaps he found it useless to counter me. A Japanese was at the mercy of a knowledgeable foreigner. The most positive thing he could do was sulk.

Setsu came outside carrying a tray of tea and cakes. She bore my son, in a string and net halter, on her back.

"Just put the tray there," I told her, "down on the verandah."

Goro, still staring ahead, bowed his head slightly to her before she returned to her kitchen. He picked up his cup and drank all his tea in two or three gulps. Then he put the glass down and wiped his brow with a handkerchief.

"You claim to have read my writing," I said to him. "Surely, then, my philosophy does not come to you as a surprise."

"May I be very blunt with you, Mr. Koizumi?"

"Yes. You may."

"That sort of philosophy makes no sense to us now. What we need from excellent people like you is guidance. You live within the confines of your illusions, and that is fine for you. I don't know. Maybe a writer needs to. But you cannot force others, who want to live here and now, to find guidance in those illusions. It is not enough for us to simply look back years later. There may be things we must do right now to guide Japan, to lead Japan onto the right path."

"Then, Goro, I see that there is no need, whatsoever, for us to continue this pretense of friendship. You certainly do not understand me in the least, though you claim to have read my writings. You, it is obvious, have ceased to be a Japanese. You are just another fawner."

He stood up and looked down at me.

"Thank you for the tea, Mr. Koizumi. I am sorry, but I did not mean to offend you in any way."

"Ah, but you have offended me."

"I am sorry."

"Your apology is worthless," I told him.

"I am not apologizing. I am only being Japanese. Remember that, Mr. Koizumi Yakumo. You, on the other hand, may never know, until the day you die, whether you were a story writer or a

Kobe

newspaperman, whether you were a European or a Japanese—or neither."

At that, Goro left. I was not to see him again. But I did subsequently learn that he abandoned Japan and went back to America. I had expected as much from him. There was no place in Japan for Japanese like Goro Izumi, and I was convinced there would be none in the future.

There was, on the other hand, a place for me. That was because I was making one for myself, one that did not depend upon the recognition—praiseful or denunciatory—of outsiders.

Our preparations were complete for putting Kobe behind us. Chamberlain had, during a waxing phase of his magnanimity, arranged for me to teach at Tokyo Imperial University, and Setsu and I were making the move with an equally shared reluctance. This did not derive from an attachment to Kobe, its sole advantage being its proximity to the temples and shrines of Kyoto. For her, Tokyo was the antithesis of her hometown life, for me, the antithesis of all life. Tokyo epitomized change: that which came after had to be good, that which went before was destined to be discarded. No single geographic spot, mass of people or symbolic entity could be more alien to my sensibilities. I even entertained the notion that Chamberlain was offering me a leprous hand in the glove of amity. As such I came more and more to value my enemies, though I had the pleasure of knowing so few of them personally, over those who swore an allegiance to me.

The night of our final day in Kobe was a moist and sweltering one, with no cooling breeze from the harbor. I tied my tiny little boy, Kazuo, onto my front with the halter. I knew that the Japanese did not use the halter in this way, swaddling them rather on their backs. This freed the women to do their daily chores. I preferred to have him face-to-face. When Japanese on the street saw me carrying him in this way, their reaction was invariably either mouth-covering laughter or blinking shock. To them I was still an *ijin*, a foreigner. I would never be a Japanese so long as I lived. This being so, my treatment of Japanese ways could fall neatly into only one of two categories. If I did something predictably foreign, evidently different, they would assume that I naturally was ignorant of the unusual Japanese mores. If I acted Japanese down to the last, most detailed, minute twist they would break their backs in bowing to my mastery of the near-impossible, and yet mistrust me for it.

Oh, I was aware of it all. I could see myself further and further, deeper and deeper, embroiled in public and private censure. Some said of me, "He cannot stop himself from being like he is." Others said, even in print, "He relishes condemnation, for it is his only salvation from bastardy." I fed off each and every word, capturing them in my mouth and turning them over with my tongue, drenching them in my resinous saliva and swallowing them one after another.

In the West Indies I had heard of a *zombi* who defied the ban on salt with live flesh and devoured the organs of humans with the aid of a gigantic salt grinder. Had I chosen to remain on Martinique instead of coming to Japan, I would no doubt have transformed myself into that very *zombi*. Think of the details of life I could have explored in that skin! But, alas, a man cannot sacrifice everything in his personality merely to be a better writer.

I walked along the alleyway, carrying my little boy, pointing out Regulus, Vega and Altair to him, until we came to an empty lot at the edge of a rise. I stood in the very center of the lot, the weeds coming up to my knees. What I said to him I wrote down immediately upon returning home. I had planned to use it in the preface of my new anthology but decided to wait for a later work. As it turned out I never published it. I record it here, then, as it came to me, word for word, on the old yellow sheet.

> This is a perfect distance for you and me. We can probably see each other better now than we shall ever be able to. Anything past this distance for us ceases to be part of the visible, the tangible, the measurable. Writers regret that, but I revel

Kobe

in it. I am constantly reducing my world and finding its definition in the remains. Writing for me is a subtraction. Once subtracted and reduced, the writer creates and re-creates his aspirations out of what is left, each day, each minute, out of the specks, puts them together in a way that makes sense only, at that very instant, to him, in that geometrically reduced space. Ah, my confinement! We—you, my precious little boy, and me—are reincarnations of what we were in our previous lives. My present one began 45 years ago on a small island in Greece, passed through years in Ireland and England and France, then wandered about the United States and the West Indies. You may ask, then, how it is that I understand my past, even from before my own time. I do. It is thanks to my hemming myself in, excluding all others, past, present and future . . . all others now except you.

Kazuo was not sleeping. He was staring, with widely opened black eyes, directly into my face.

"I wish that I had your eyes from now on," I told him, bouncing him gently up and down as I had seen his mother do.

I was convinced that he was contributing something to me, that there was nothing whatsoever stopping him from being my father and I from being his infant son. It was not the influence of the stars above our heads which made me sense this. I could see them no longer, for I cared nothing for them. It was his pupils. I would inherit them. They would be my pupils from now on.

Once home I put Kazuo on top of my futon and lay my head on his chest, as if it were true.

1904   Tokyo

I stepped off the Ginza into a large bookshop. It was snowing lightly on a mid-January morning, and the district seemed to be just emerging from the bare New Year. The "fashionable" people—no doubt the crowd that loiters at the Metropole Hotel in Tsukiji—were ambling about on the "fashionable" street only to present themselves to others considered by them less fashionable. There was nothing left of Japan in this city but a competition of masks.

On the eye-level shelf near the front of the shop was a book with a handwritten advertisement wrapper: "Newly Published! Key to the Unpicking of the Japanese Mind. *One Hundred More Exceedingly Queer Things About the Japanese.*" Below that shelf I noticed some of my own works. I counted them and was about to upbraid the proprietor for carrying and displaying only six of my nine books on Japanese life, but he was engaged in an elevated discussion of aesthetics and commerce, the balance of which had been crudely tampered with by the Japanese during my fourteen years' residence. The discussion was with an unusually tall stout and red-haired Englishwoman. The height of the proprietor himself did not reach five feet, bringing his nose to mid-corset. They were not so much talking to each other as in each other's directions, up and down, in this case.

The woman was apparently interested in purchasing some of the woodblock prints stacked on the shop's wooden counter.

"Look, my good man," she was saying. "These are simply not well painted. I am afraid that the price you ask is not appropriate."

The proprietor spoke moderately fluent English but with a heavy Japanese accent.

"These are not painted, madame," he said, pronouncing the appellation in the French manner, with emphasis on the second syllable. "They are printed."

"I see. But surely only a technical difference. The fact remains that they are not artistically worthy."

"I am not sure that I understand you, madame. I realize that these do not compare favorably with the great works of art of Europe. But they are created by some of my country's most famous artists of the past. Here are prints by Utamaro, Hiroshige and Kunisada."

He rifled through the stack of prints on the counter.

"Nonetheless, famous in Japan, yes, but are they known in England or Europe? Not in the least. To be of universal value art must be recognized in Europe, the home of all art."

He was now standing virtually up against her and craning his neck to see past her swelling bosom to her face. I was certain that all he could see from there would be the tip of her nose, which was shaped like the cutting edge of a chisel. "If madame values our art so little, then why is madame so interested in purchasing so many?"

"Oh, mere souvenirs of the voyage. But I shall not pay unfair prices for such souvenirs, let me tell you that. This is outrageous and, furthermore, would never happen in England or Europe, where booksellers are honest and conscientious in their dealings. Never have I encountered such underhanded behavior in a shop before."

Tokyo

The woman was now glaring down at the proprietor, her chin resting against, and cleaving, her chest.

"Madame, I know that the ways of the men of my country are base and hateful. But I assure you that I am not such. I have been in the United States of America and have seen with my own eyes the upright manners of gentlemen of trade and commerce."

"The United States of America? It stands to reason," she said, flicking through the stack of prints. "Look at this. Look at these small little Japanese men in this picture. They are not even drawn in perspective. In our art, which the entire world, including you Japanese, I might add, recognizes as superior, the smaller people should be placed in the background, that is to say in the distance, as it were. Such is art, my good man."

"But in this print," said the proprietor, ducking under the woman's outstretched arm and removing the print from the top of the stack, "here you can see big men beside little men. This little man is not important in rank, so he is small. How can you tell in European art which man is less important so readily?"

The woman, visibly exasperated at her inability to drum what was to her the most elementary aesthetic sense into the mind of the little Japanese man at her waist, opened her purse, took several notes from her wallet and slapped them on the counter.

"Very well then, wrap up the lot. But I have never been so insulted in all my days. You have another think coming, my good man."

The proprietor, despite his excellent grasp of English, obviously misunderstood this final phrase.

"Oh, thank you. I am so sorry, madame, if I disturbed your days. Please forgive my unschooled ways. I want to have another think coming. Please, please, anytime you want to give it, please do not hesitate to hightail it into my shop again, as those Americans say. They are so kind. Please."

His neck was bent back a full ninety degrees, and he was smiling toward the woman's red head, showing her unashamedly the few pointy teeth he had left. The woman stepped around him, and he rotated his head obediently to follow her, a moon trapped in the gravitational grip of its superior planet.

"I shall return later to fetch them," said the woman. "I have had my fill of this for now."

As she exited she managed to throw a disapproving glance at me, as if I too were somehow culpable in what was to her a brutally shylocked transaction. The proprietor looked forlorn and upset. He was, in his own eyes, a servant who had unwittingly insulted his master, a docile monkey in a sideshow cage who had angered his keeper, a helpless animal who would choose death from starvation over recrimination. Such were the men of Tokyo. They had forsworn their past, taking the Occidental oath. Foreign visitors were talking about the vanishing Japan. But I knew it to be long gone already, leaving only the pathetic and alms-seeking to form a shadow.

"May I help you, sir?" he said, approaching me from the counter, no doubt prepared for another such reviling.

"*Kekko desu,*" I said, "No, thank you."

"Oh, you speak Japanese. And you are dressed like a Japanese. Are you an American, sir?"

"Sayonara."

I walked out of his shop, boarded a rickshaw and ordered the runner to take me to the campus of Tokyo Imperial University. It was snowing more heavily now, and I pulled up the collar of the woolen overcoat that Setsu had bought me for the Christmas of 1903. I had been thinking of my father on that day. I had fathered four children myself, but, except for Kazuo, felt only the mildest emotions toward them. I had not been my father's eldest. That boy had died shortly after my birth. A couple of years after I came into the world, my younger brother, whom I never cared to

Tokyo

contact, emerged, followed by my half-sisters. Would my father have laughed to see his son turned into a Japanese? It would have been beyond his niggard imagination. I wanted him to see me just once, not huddled and humpbacked on the seat of the rickshaw in Tokyo, but proudly dressed in upper and lower crested formal *hakama*, attending an elegant banquet. All of the invitees, as is the custom, are announced upon entrance: Mr. and Mrs. Ito, the Marquis and Marchioness Kurosagi—Occidentals to the right, Japanese and other Asiatics to the left, and last of all, son of the proud and restless army surgeon Charles Hearn, Mr. Yakumo Koizumi, who arrives with his hair bobbed in a tea-whisk braid and in full-blown Japanese formal attire. And no sooner does Mr. Koizumi arrive than he is faced, in his perpetual wink, with a unique dilemma: to walk to the right or to walk to the left, while being watched closely by this crowd of cummerbund-wearing, bemedaled nobility. And I, Myriad Clouds Minor Stream, lift up the hem of my black-heron-crested *hakama* and walk straight up the middle, do you understand, straight up the middle!

"Are you all right, sir?" asked the runner.

I had not realized myself that I was sitting there, as if atop all Tokyo, laughing my blooming head off.

The students had become used to me. Or, at least if they had not, there was no telling shock in their expressions. I wore my old wide-brimmed hat, the very same one I had worn since my New Orleans days, and a brown kimono. But it being winter, I could not forego my shoes, though I often wore white *tabi* socks under them. I liked the feeling of the soft fabric between my big and second toes.

My routine upon entering the classroom was known throughout the campus. I would sit on the desk rather than at it, remove my hat and pipe and begin the lesson by reciting poetry, everything from Coleridge and Poe to *The Children's Treasury of English Song*.

Roger Pulvers

> "O Father! I hear the church-bells ring
> O say what may it be?"
> "'Tis a fog-bell on the rock-bound coast!"
> And he sailed for open sea.

During one lesson I had placed my pipe on the chalk rack and forgotten it. Some minutes before the lesson's end I searched for it around and in my hat, on, in and under the desk. Unable to find it, I sat down, devoid of all strength in my body, and wept in front of my students. I quickly realized the state I had fallen into, raised my chin, wiped my eye on the brim of my hat and told them that I had just recalled my father, who had himself died at sea. This moved some of them to tears. Such was my power as a teacher of university students. The cleverest of teachers were those who had the ability to change the subject suddenly. As my students stood up to bow to me, I finished them off.

> "O Father! I see a gleaming light
> O say what may it be?"
> But the father answer'd never a word
> A frozen corpse was he.

I had all of them weeping now.

After the students had left, I sat alone at my desk, reached back for my pipe, as if I had known it was there all the while, lit it and chuckled mercilessly to myself, into the smoke that I was creating.

In late February, as I had observed those past eight years, the warm balsam days of a false spring overtook Tokyo. I stopped under a single cherry blossom tree to inspect its buds. The mathematics of the buds of this particular tree did intrigue me. I could see this tree as I looked out from the window of my classroom. It was an exceptionally tall one, and the buds on the uppermost branch could very nearly be reached from my window.

I had brought a bench from my room to a spot under the tree, hopped onto it and was examining a bud with my magnifying glass when I noticed a student of mine named Hirota nearby. He stood together with a young woman. They were watching me with intense curiosity.

"What do you think, Hirota?" I asked him in a loud voice. "When would you say this bud will cease to exist?"

No doubt embarrassed by being addressed outside of the classroom by his instructor, Hirota lowered his gaze to the ground. The young woman beside him lowered her gaze as well. I jumped down from the bench and went to them.

"You are my best student, Hirota. Tell me, which author do you find the most satisfying? And, is this young lady your friend?"

Hirota continued to look downward.

"Hmm?" I said.

"I am most interested in Lafcadio Hearn, sir," he said in the softest of voices.

"A most polite reply. Now, as to the second of my questions?"

He was silent.

"Hmm? I did not hear you."

Again he said nothing.

"Yes, I am," said the young woman. "We are lovers."

Hirota's neck stiffened. He pursed his lips tightly, flushed a dark crimson and stared at the woman through the corner of his eyes, frozen in timid rage.

"I see. That is being most forthright, I must say. Young women in Matsue, where I first lived in Japan, would never say such things."

"Matsue?" she said, looking at Hirota, who was now, poor fellow, more embarrassed than ever. He looked like he was going to faint on the spot. "Professor, Hirota would like to ask you something."

"By all means. Please feel free to talk openly with me. Are you two getting married and asking me to be the go-between? If so, I would be honored and delighted. I am a born go-between."

"No!" said Hirota, clenching his fists, then suddenly relaxing and lifting his head. "Sir. We students in your class are planning to have an excru . . . an ex-crus. . ."

"An excursion?"

"Yes, that is it. An excur . . . Some of us will take our friends, e.g., this one here."

"Very fine. But one does not say 'e.g,' Hirota. One only writes it."

"Oh, I am sorry, sir."

"Don't apologize. And?"

"And?" he repeated.

"And what about this excursion?"

"Oh yes, of course. Sir, we are hoping that you will accom . . . acc . . . I mean, go with us. To Hakone. In May. Please forgive my naughty behavior for asking such a thing."

"Not naughty at all. I should be delighted to accompany you, all of you. Thank you very much, Hirota, and . . . What is your name?"

"My name is Emi Inagaki."

I had, from as far back as fourteen years' memory went, been gently repulsed by Japanese women who clearly despised their station and made a point of the display. But, for some reason, Emi Inagaki was pleasing to me. I suppose this was due to a fondness for Hirota. I wanted my own little son, Kazuo, to be like him; and I wished—against the mathematics which I had but a moment before been observing—that it could not be in the future.

Tokyo

Setsu came into my room.

"Your dinner is ready," she said.

I told her to put it beside my desk. My desk, a piano keyboard of white cards and old pipes, had no place for it. In addition I was not yet ready to eat. Setsu brought the tray to the desk, kneeled and placed it on the tatami mat.

"I am eating downstairs," she said.

"Fine."

I returned to my book. The chilly weather had returned in early March, and my eye was pounding like a country drum. I was working on a book I would call *The Romance of the Milky Way*.

"What time is it?" I asked Setsu as she was about to leave my room.

"Ten o'clock. I have waited to have my own dinner, but I will go ahead with it now."

"No one asked you to wait for me."

"The baby has finally gone to sleep," she said, turning her back and descending the staircase.

Setsu returned forty-five minutes later. I chastised her for interrupting me again. I was writing a chapter on war. The entire world was privy to every alleged Japanese transgression outside of the empire, yet arrogantly unaware of the peacefulness reigning within these islands' shores. Their victories in the Sino-Japanese war some ten years ago gave great impetus to their shipping, and Mr. Iwasaki's Mitsubishi Mail Steamship Company, the largest and most impressive enterprise, had carried troops of the Imperial Army whenever called upon to do so. The needs of the government and its businesses were inseparable. This bond lent a rightful status to Japanese pride. A mere 739 Japanese lives were lost in battle in that war, and though this had to be added to the 3,148 who died from disease, primarily the Chinese cholera, it constituted a small price to pay for genuine national dignity.

"I thought I told you to leave me be," I said to her.

"I am sorry. I noticed how chilly it had become, and I came in only to light the hibachi for you."

I rubbed my eye, which was now aching intolerably and felt like a large hard stone embedded in a socket.

"Thank you."

"There is no need to thank me," she said.

I put my pen down, lit one of my old briars, and looked down at the dinner tray, untouched, beside my desk.

"I know, Setsu, that many say you married a *yabanjin*, a barbarian. Do you, too, think this? I certainly would not blame you for it."

"A *yabanjin*? I do not think so," she said, stoking the cold ash in the hibachi. "I think I married a Japanese."

I motioned for her to come to me, which she did, and I sat her on my lap, closing my one eye. A strange Japanese, this woman, married off when still young and taken from her distant province to this so-foreign city. What would she look like on her deathbed? I did not know how to ask her that. I could not find the words in Japanese. I could have said, "What will you look like when you die? I want to see you then." But this would have been misunderstood. She held my head against her body, and I stopped myself from weeping again. I had promised myself that I would not break down that day, as I had on every other in recent months.

I was awake at five the next morning. I went downstairs to find Kazuo playing by himself. Setsu and the other children were apparently still asleep. He had his arithmetic book in front of him, but instead of studying it, was crouched by the sliding papered door poking his finger through it and making holes. I watched him for some moments in silence until he turned around, saw me and put both his hands behind his back. I went down on my hands and knees, crawled over the tatami to him, stuck the index finger of my right hand in my mouth and, extricating it, poked a huge hole in the tautly stretched paper. This sent Kazuo into gales of laughter, and we rivaled each other to see who could make the loudest and cleanest rows of holes evenly across the door.

When there was as much air as paper in the door I fell back on my behind, and we both shook with laughter. It was then that I noticed Setsu standing in the doorway. She was observing her "two little boys," as she often called us. The maid behind her was covering her mouth with both her hands.

"So you see, Kazuo," I said to my son in a deep resonant tone, one perfected by me for my students to lend authority to my words, "each square in the door will have either an even or an odd number of holes." This, I reckoned, would attach reason to our mischief.

"What's this, papa?" he asked, pointing to a picture in his arithmetic book, obviously taking the more likely ploy of distraction.

"Hm?"

"This here. What is this in the book? It is a *kani*, isn't it?"

"Yes. But speak English. It is a crab."

"It is a crab," he said in English.

"Good. Now, how many crabs are there?"

"One *kani*, papa."

"One crab."

"One crab," he repeated, looking admirably serious.

I turned my eye to Setsu and smiled at her.

"Good. Now give papa this pencil. Here, I will draw another one. Now, how many crabs are there?"

"Two *kani*, papa."

"No! Two crabs!" I shouted at him.

"Two crabs!" he shouted back.

"Good!"

"Good!"

I then drew a picture of two fishermen with narrow bands around their heads tied in a knot at the temple.

"How many fishermen, eh?"

"Two, papa."

"Two what?"

"Shermen."

"Fish-ermen."

"Fish-ermen."

"Good."

"Good."

"Now. Papa will cut the heads off the two fishermen with these *hasami* and put the heads and bodies in a row."

"Not *hasami*, papa. Scissors."

"All right, all right. Here. Now, look at it. Concentrate, Kazuo. How many fishermen do you see now?"

Kazuo did not answer. He merely looked into my face with a puzzled expression.

"How many? Look here. One, two, three, four. Four fishermen."

He stared down at the two bodies and the two heads in a row. It was obvious that he could not see how this represented four fishermen.

How much of a teacher's success, I wondered, lay in pauses and tones of voice? I detested the need to explain myself to others. How could one explain outlines? Providing the details of the concrete interior would not do it. Reducing everything over and

Tokyo

over again until only lines were left was the only way—the instant before those lines flashed once, burned an impression like a brand on the eye, then, fleeting, disappeared once and for all. The truth of the matter consisted in its having existed a single time only.

There was a changing atmosphere about the city of Tokyo. One could sense it evolving with the days. Pride in their nation and its achievements was rendering the Japanese increasingly stubborn and patriotic. The reaction to these changes of the foreign "community" amused me. They had become so fond of their quaint and humble Japanese. They did not want to see the Japanese standing up on their own two feet. They preferred to see them on their knees, prostrate before towering white-man civilization.

It had recently become law that no photographs were to be permitted in officially designated forbidden zones around forts and places under military ban. The foreigners smarted. Their freedom to "roam these parts freely" was being curtailed. This ban was an insult directly to them, as they interpreted it. I suggested to one of them, a doltish Belgian *bugaku*, or court dance, scholar, that all Japan should be put under such prohibition and that *ijin*—Belgian *bugaku* scholars in particular—be forbidden entry into shrines, gardens, and other sacred spots. He called me "dangerous." I had never been so pleased by innuendo in my entire life and regretted only that he had not said it in print.

My reputation at the university had divided camps. On the one hand there were those few freewheeling spirits who took in my eccentricities as inspiration. Stories of how I mixed salt into my coffee instead of sugar, of how I refused to use the telephone, that instrument of inhumanity, of how in restaurants I left my table before being served convinced that I had finished my meal—these petty and personal habits merely augmented my aura to some. The tales about me were, needless to say, entirely true. With the majority, however, my quirks appeared as sheer and obstinate perversity. Some among them were intent on routing me from my position at the university. As for me, I preferred temple groves to academic ones. The latter had no cemeteries to walk about on gray evenings unless, of course, one counted one's distinguished European and American colleagues among—to use the beloved phrase of the West Indies—the living dead.

I was sitting on my desk in the classroom. It was spring, and the cherry blossoms were in full bloom, but I was doing my best not to notice them. I had made it a point to begin every lesson with questions. I knew that my students, being Japanese, would be reluctant to ask questions of their teacher. By starting each lesson with a fixed question period, I obliged them to do it, if only for form's sake.

"Please tell us, professor, about the Norwegian playwright, Henrik Ibsen," asked one of them. "Do you judge highly his writings?"

I jumped off the desk and paced the platform it stood on.

"It is far better," I said, "to discuss that literature which will be lasting. All of this experimentation is but a minute flicker compared to the raging fires of eighteenth-century English literature and the nineteenth-century French. I advise you to concern yourselves with those things which will be with us forever."

I ended my little speech with my back to them, pausing a good three minutes before turning around. It was as obvious to them as it was to me that I knew nothing about the Norwegian playwright Henrik Ibsen, that my isolation in Matsue, Kumamoto and Kobe had created stupefying gaps in my knowledge of contemporary European letters. At such times I found myself becoming stiff and pompous, just a blind bluff from yet another stern white and intimidating face. Before the Japanese, a stern bluff was a simple trick.

What could I teach my students by merely speaking my language? I had to say something which would give them a genuine impression of the outside world, something they could hardly glean from the peripheral representatives of the Occident forced

Tokyo

into their midst. Should I give them, I wondered, examinations full of useless Japanese facts, impressing them with my command of them? What is the tallest mountain in Japan? I am ashamed of you, Onishi. It is most definitely not Fujiyama. It is Formosa's Niitakayama, formerly named Mt. Morrison, at 14,350 feet, a full two thousand feet higher than Fujiyama. The Japanese see ignorance as shame. It is their most hideous trait. How could I demonstrate to them that, all knowledge being illusory, such ignorance was a man's glory? The only way, I finally realized, was by example.

"Listen to me," I told them, now standing with my customary slouch between my desk and them. "Do you want to know facts? Do you wish to learn about the true nature of 'my' civilization, as it is so honorably referred to in Japan? You have heard me speak in this room of great English poets such as Byron and Coleridge, writers such as Lamb and Swinburne, whom I believe to be still alive. Do you know what made them into poets? Flogging. That quintessentially English practice which another poet, Thomas Gray, called 'the schoolmaster's joy.' Joy. Do you understand?"

I went to the blackboard and drew a whip in chalk. Drawing had always been my forte, and I took pains to describe the twists in the cat as faithfully as possible.

"George IV, my boys—I think you will follow this—here is what he himself wrote, the King of Hanover and the United Kingdom of Great Britain and Ireland, boys."

I copied the king's words regarding flagellation on the blackboard.

> Delightful sport! whose never failing charm
> Makes young blood tingle, and keeps old blood warm.

"Not that this applies to your aging professor. I want you to know that I am being strictly objective in explaining the esoterica of my civilization, as you call it. And since all of you are men, I think it not inappropriate to mention that Lord Byron himself, that greatest of all English poets, had incest with his sister. Do not condemn us, however. Merely know that you have already learned everything in these long thirty-seven years of Meiji that you are ever to learn from Europe. I am included in this. You have nothing to learn from me. I am ignorant and I, in your native dress, bow down before you."

I went down on my hands and knees on the platform in front of them. This had the result of embarrassing the dickens out of them. Another result was surely to be a report to the university authorities, thus bringing my professorial neck that much closer to the chopping block. Would I have the honor of being the first "invited Occidental scholar" to be given his papers? "Not at all what we expected when we hired you, old boy!" God, how my loathing for England had only grown in vehemence and proportion over the years!

I stood up abruptly and broke into prolonged laughter. Relieved by this, for it indicated to them that what they had heard and seen was but a play, a bitterly told farce entitled "European Decadence as Described by the World's Most Possessed Naturalized Japanese," the students laughed heartily with me.

"Thank you, thank you," I said, taking a bow, this time on my feet. "Now, you see, we must be informal with each other. If the Occident has a gift to give Japan, it is informality. Informality breeds equality, or at least provides a rickety platform for it. Ask me a question, please. Let us pretend that you are the teachers and I the pupil. You may learn something that way. Come along, don't be shy. Hirota, what about you? Do you not want to ask me something, eh?"

Hirota stood.

"Good lad."

"Sir?"

"Remember, you are the teacher and I, the pupil. Kindly dispense with the honorifics."

Tokyo

"I have a question for you," he said, readjusting his posture. "Do you think that Henry James will change his cizi . . . I mean . . . cizi . . . citizenship . . . and become a British subject? Is it permissible that I ask you that?"

"Do not ask my permission. Of course it is permissible. What do I care if he changes his citizenship or not, eh? What is the difference in such a thing?"

"Um, yes . . . but, it made a big difference to you, Professor Hearn."

For a moment he looked terrified. Had he taken my invitation to informality too far? Japanese had difficulty adopting informality without it turning sour into rudeness.

"You are absolutely right, Hirota. Yes. It did make a difference to me. But it hardly means that it would have the same meaning for Mr. Henry James, who presumably will, unlike me, retain his original name, though, who knows, the British might ask him to hyphenate it."

"I do not understand, sir."

"That is a beginning to becoming enlightened, Hirota."

"I have one more question."

"Marvelous. There is still a moment or two left for us."

"What about your writing?"

"My writing?"

"Your own writing, as Yakumo Koizumi. Will it remain, like Byron and Coleridge's did, after your death?"

I went to the blackboard and erased my whip and George IV's poem. Once again I gazed at them, leaning against the blackboard's rail. Hirota sat down. The bells tolled outside, indicating the end of the hour.

"Saved by the bell—or could it be divine intervention. Whichever it is, I have no answer for you, Hirota, except that my own writing is . . . just an echo. Good day."

The boys stood simultaneously and bowed. I was so moved by my own histrionics and the providence of a timely bell that I walked out like that, chin in the air and arms swinging freely, forgetting my hat on the desk. It was the first and last time I was to do that. The next day it was in the same spot, untouched by anyone, as if it belonged there forever, as if it symbolized my presence in that room better than I could myself.

Setsu put out her hand shyly for me to take it and walk with her. She had never made such a gesture in public. We had left the four children at home with the maid and were walking down the street to the public bath, she holding two small pine tubs with towels in them. I was not about to take her hand, even if it would please her.

"You would never have dared to do something so crudely borrowed as that in Matsue or Kumamoto," I said to her, striding ahead.

It was customary for Japanese wives to walk three paces behind their husbands. I felt, however, that I had to teach Setsu a lesson. Life in Tokyo had removed some of her natural defenses against impropriety. I rushed some twenty feet ahead of her. I reached the entrance of the public bathhouse and waited there for her. But she did not come. I retraced my steps, finding her crouching at the spot where I had left her behind.

"This is nothing to cry over," I told her.

"I am not crying over this. I am crying over what has occurred for more than thirteen years."

I crouched beside her, though it was difficult at my age to do so while wearing clogs.

Tokyo

"I ask you to forgive me, Setsu. I am unable to change. But I certainly do know how difficult a man I am. I need to be this way so that I may write. Perhaps you are paying the price for marrying a man who was alone until he was forty."

"In a few years I too will be forty. I have given you four children."

Having said this she began to weep, burying her face in a towel.

"There is nothing that I can do about it now."

I helped her up and, though the thought alone repulsed me, I took her hand and walked slowly beside her to the bathhouse.

I had been in many public bathhouses in Japan, primarily in the country. Most of these had mixed bathing, although the combination of shortsightedness on my part and flat-chestedness on that of most Japanese women had rendered the custom of negligible significance to me. I was virtually always peering through steam in any case. Perhaps this partially accounted for my lack of interest in the mere description of fact.

I took my tub and towel from Setsu and we entered our separate sections, Tokyo having abandoned the "rustic customs of the provinces," such as mixed bathing. I dropped my kimono to the floor and put it in a basket. I took off my *shita-obi* loincloth and carried it into the bathing area with me. In Matsue I had become accustomed to using my loincloth as a towel to wash with. Here such a practice was deemed "primitive." I relished such appearances, for they showed the Japanese that their bygone practices would be preserved, if only by this single out-of-step stranger.

I washed my body with my loincloth and soap, the gaze of every man in the bathhouse fixed on me. I then rinsed my loincloth thoroughly of the suds and stepped into the hot water, placing my loincloth, folded, on top of my head and singing a popular *naniwabushi* ballad with a strained voice and a high pitch in my heavily accented Japanese.

> A chilly autumn night
> The sky dyed, awash in blue

Roger Pulvers

> And on all the sky-lit paths
> The black shadows of the pampas grass
> Pierced by the boom-boom-boom
> Of the giant *tanuki* raccoon dog, pounding his belly

The entire bathhouse, on both male and female sides, was plunged into silence. I, of course, could not see Setsu sitting in the water on the other side of the partition. But I could imagine what was going through her mind at that moment. I felt sorry for her. Yes, I did. But there was nothing to be done about it. I had taken her name for life.

I made a fatal mistake, succumbing to admiration. A man who was writing occasional religious notices in the English-language daily—I called his notices "articles of faith"—telephoned me at the university with an invitation to his home.

"I am anxious," he said, "to introduce you to an ardent admirer of your work, a writer in his own right."

Thus I found myself victimized yet again by praise-mongering foreigners, a guild of sycophants who brush by one only to spread the particles of gold dust onto themselves. I had always feared such friends more than any enemy. They absorbed my time, and I was an emptied vessel for weeks after.

The house of the Reverend Gerald Winter was a palace in Shirogane such as only the wealthiest and most long-established Japanese families could aspire to own. Not that either the good reverend or his righteous mission were well off. They depended on contributions and parcels from "the home states," as he fondly called them.

"The land here was acquired for a song," he told me shortly after I arrived and spilled out the customary niceties learned in America, where not lavishing words on one's host's domicile was a crime worthy of ostracism. "Apparently after the Meiji Restoration some Buddhist or somebody like that had decided that the land around here was inhabited by ghosts. They sold it to our church and probably considered it a curse on us at the same time. Ghosts, can you imagine?"

"Yes, I can," I said, coming down the wide spiral staircase after inspecting, at Mrs. Winter's insistence, the "totally modern washroom."

It was two o'clock in the afternoon, and I should have feigned fever, excused myself and left on the spot. But the Winters' eleven-year-old daughter, Louise, was fascinated by me. She had read a book of mine, *Shadowings*, and asked me that stock question which, when coming from an adult, I ignore by flashing my bottom teeth and bulging out my Cyclops eye.

"What prompted you to write that book, Mr. Koizumi?" she asked, her tone so precocious and fresh that the question disarmed me of my rancor.

"What prompted you to ask?" I replied.

"Curiosity, I suppose," she said, furrowing her brow. "I loved the chapter on Japanese female names. I never thought about names in that way. It led me to examine American names. They all have a meaning too, don't they?"

"Many of them do."

"Now, enough chatter," said Mrs. Winter, whose first name I had not been told. "Supper is ready. The good professor is a busy man, and we are most honored by his presence in our humble home."

"Where is the writer-admirer of mine?"

"Yes, yes," said the reverend. "He is expected, and I can only offer you my apologies for his tardiness."

One of their servants, a frail Japanese man of about sixty, came through the swinging doors from the kitchen holding, in gloved hands, a large silver lidded soup tureen.

"Not yet, boy," said the reverend. "I told you I would indicate to you when we were ready to start."

The servant bowed and returned to the kitchen. A loud knocking was heard at the front door.

"That must be the gentleman now," said Mrs. Winter, leaving the dining room. There was a long silence, during which the reverend laughed in embarrassment and winked at me. His wife came back into the room, followed by a middle-aged man.

"Professor Hearn, it is my pleasure to introduce to you a man of your own profession, Mr. Walter Pectopah."

"How do you do?" I said, bowing my head.

He walked toward me and put out his hand.

"We have met once before," he said.

"I am sorry. I do not recall it."

"Oh, it was many years ago, on the road leading to Matsue. I was looking for Lafcadio Hearn. I think that in your heart you had already become Yakumo Koizumi."

"Yes, now I remember," I said, shaking his hand, yet unable to recall the encounter.

A tall, white-haired man entered the dining room.

"I left my mackintosh in the closet by the front door. Is that all right, Mrs. Winter?"

"Of course it is. And now, a gentleman without whom neither of you would exist, a publisher, and an eminent one indeed, from America, Mr. Peter Butler. Mr. Butler, Professor Hearn, Mr. Walter Pectopah. Do I pronounce that correctly?"

"It has been pronounced in so many ways," said Pectopah.

"Your reputation in America is formidable," Butler said to me.

"Formidably what?" I replied.

"Hmm . . . just formidable. Is that not what all writers desire? Notoriety?"

Tokyo

I smiled at him and turned my head slightly to the left so that the white of my eyeball faced him squarely on.

"Let us sit down, gentlemen, please," said the reverend, indicating our places at the dining table. I was seated opposite Louise. Once again the old servant entered, carrying the tureen as before.

"Who told you to come in, huh?" said Mrs. Winter. "What do you Britishers say, professor? It's the 'devil's own job' to get reliable servants these days, is that it?"

Without replying, I grinned and stared at Mrs. Winter.

"I must admit," said Butler to me, "I have long looked forward to meeting America's most famous Japanese."

"Japan's most famous Greek Irishman, please," I said.

"Well, be that as it may," said the reverend, "I am glad that you could all come together today under out humble roof."

I could see that the swinging doors to the kitchen were open by a crack. The old servant and a young Japanese kitchen maid were peering through it. The kitchen maid was giggling.

"It appears that your domestic staff," I said, "have never seen a Caucasian dressed as a Japanese before, though no doubt they have seen many Japanese dressed as Caucasians. They might be doubly amused if I showed them my Japanese long johns. Wonderful things, these *momohiki*."

I lifted my leg to the height of the table and pulled the hem of my kimono up to my thigh. The swinging door immediately shut, and we could all hear the muffled sounds of giggling coming from the kitchen.

"You wear those?" said Pectopah. "In all my years in Japan I have never seen a foreigner do that."

"Many, however, do wear socks with holes in them like these, I trust," I told him, lifting my foot to the level of the table and, resting my heel on its edge, removing my shoe.

The reverend cleared his throat.

"Perhaps it is time to say grace," he said. "Mrs. Winter will lead us today."

"Why, thank you, Gerald," she said, blushing.

"What's so funny about Mr. Koizumi wearing those Japanese things?" asked Louise. "I don't get it."

"Shush, Louise," said her father. "Now, your mother will say grace."

All heads were bowed, all, that is, except mine. I dipped my index finger into the glass of cold water in front of me, closed my right eye and rubbed my wet fingertip over its lid.

The reverend's study was virtually pitch-black. Only the outline of his body could be seen with perfect clarity, as if its single curving line were a border between the worlds of light and dark. He lit a kerosene lamp made of red transparent glass. I stood in the study's doorway and observed him. He noticed a book of Japanese woodblock prints, bound loosely in cloth and thread, on his desk. He looked up and saw me.

"Oh, Mr. Hearn, is this the book which you brought for me?"

"Yes it is, reverend. That is the one."

"I am much obliged to you, sir."

He opened the book and slowly leafed through its delicate pages, cocking his head from time to time to see the prints properly. I took a few steps toward him. The prints all retained their spectacular original colors. The reverend began to notice—I could tell by watching his twitching nose and quivering lips—that the prints were becoming progressively erotic. One by one they revealed a section of white-powdered neck or curling toes coming out from a dark purple or floral-patterned kimono.

I stood now some ten feet from him. He cleared his throat and turned another page. He stopped and lowered his head slightly to examine one of the prints.

Tokyo

"Ah, that is the one I especially wanted you to see," I said to him.

It was a print of a woman with wildly disheveled hair lying naked on her back. Between her spread legs was a large octopus, its bulging eyes peering over her belly, its thick lips licking her genitals, two of the tips of its tentacles touching her nipples and another her pink bulging exposed clitoris.

"It is called 'The Dream of the Fisherman's Wife,'" I said. "Rather realistic, wouldn't you say?"

"Uh, yes, I would," he muttered, unable to take his eyes off the picture.

Just then the kerosene lamp exploded, sending slivers of glass over the desk and onto the picture. The reverend lifted up his right hand. It was bleeding profusely. He held it by the wrist with his left hand, an expression of extreme gasping pain on his face. His mouth was pried wide open, his teeth protruding as those of a de-fleshed skull. Blood from his hand fell in large drops onto the picture.

I opened my right eye. I was back at the table, sitting with the others as a moment before.

"Amen," said Mrs. Winter, finishing her prayer.

The others lifted their heads, peering at the reverend. "I think we can begin now," he said. "Thank you, Lord, for bringing our friends together."

The servant entered as before, carrying the silver tureen. He looked at the reverend and his wife with a most timid and obsequious squint.

"That's all right," said Mrs. Winter, nodding her head and smiling benevolently at him with pursed lips.

Another Japanese servant, a young woman, appeared with a large pitcher—the American kind, round and rippled, as if made of corrugated glass. A small amount of the fruit juice in it was poured into each glass except for Louise's.

"This is Mrs. Winter's own home brew," sniggered the reverend, covering his mouth and raising an eyebrow.

When my glass was poured I drank its contents immediately and held it up to the servant girl, who was still beside me. She exchanged glances with Mrs. Winter, who nodded imperceptibly, and poured me more. I kept pushing my glass up against the lip of the pitcher until it was full.

"We do not drink in actuality," said the reverend.

"Oh, neither do I," I said, my mouth to the glass. "Not in actuality."

"I mean, what I mean is, it is not the Lord's way."

My mouth full of liquid, glued to the glass, I shook my head.

"Mrs. Winter puts a few extra raisins into the juice and, after a while, well, oh my dear, it becomes a trifle intoxicating, if you know what I mean," he said, chuckling.

I finished drinking my raisin-fermented brew and looked down at the steaming bowl put before me. I reached into my inside coat pocket, brought out my magnifying glass and examined the soup's contents at close range.

In the living room after supper, during which I said not a single word, though asked a number of penetrating questions, I stood by the mantelpiece smoking one of the good reverend's cigars. Pectopah, his chin jutting out like the anal fin of a shark, his nostrils flared, his elbow grandiosely lodged on the mantelpiece as if posing for an early Victorian oil, suddenly turned to me.

"Did I ever tell you of my Slavic origins?" he asked.

"How could you have? Was that Slavic or slavish? I am certainly no linguist, but I understand they share a root."

Tokyo

"Mr. Hearn. You once described this country as 'an unknown fairy-world full of beautiful riddles,' if I quote you precisely."

"As precisely as I recall it myself," I said. "Oh, Reverend Winter, are these cigars sent from your mission headquarters in the home states?"

"Yes, as a matter of fact, they are," he said, glancing toward me and away from Butler, with whom he was engaged in heated discussion on the settee.

"You are well provided for, aren't you? Is this a form of divine providence as well?"

Butler stood and joined us by the mantel.

"Do you still believe that, I mean, that this is a fairy-world?" asked Pectopah. "What is so beautiful, I would like to know, about these warmongering little monkeys? And bear in mind, if you will, I am no fleeting globetrotter, but have lived in this country for the better part of two decades."

"Well, I don't know. These monkeys seem to have achieved in thirty years what the Occident took three hundred to create. And they have retained their spirit in the bargain."

"Spirit?" said the reverend, now making a fourth, as if this were but a clever little game of verbal whist by an unlit hearth. "More like a pack of superstitions parading as patriotism. They have made life impossible for all foreigners, discriminated against us with their vile narrow laws, been superficially polite to us while excluding us all the while from their every inner circle. They pretend to tolerate God, the only true God, but they just let it wash all over them, like their lewd bathhouse soap. It may make them look clean, but the core is filth, rot and incapable of purification save by a forced salvation."

"Their laws have merely redressed all of the unfairness which was imposed upon them when America forced them open," I said.

"I suppose that you are against that too, Mr. Hearn," said Butler.

"Against what, opening up? Not in itself. But until only a few years ago, 1899 to be exact, when privileges were curtailed, foreigners in Japan were able to act as if they lived in their own little republics with their own little laws. No, my friends, one Shanghai in Asia is enough."

The old servant brought along a tray with hot coffee. We each took a cup and saucer. I drank mine down, placing the empty cup and saucer on the mantelpiece.

"No Oriental race has ever given into Christianity," I said. "Why should they?"

"Now hold your horses," said the reverend, his cup trembling in his hand. "We have increased the number of people baptized since 1872 a hundredfold."

"Don't ask him, gentlemen, how many were baptized in 1872."

"Whoa. Just you hold on a minute here. Now you're going too far, for a guest or for anybody. The Salvation Army was established here in 1895."

"God save our souls."

He seemed not to hear my interruption and continued talking, his face turning pink and his cup shaking more audibly against its saucer.

"We have done much charitable work here, sir, and are deeply appreciated by all and sundry."

"Didn't the Japanese burn and torture Christians here in the seventeenth century?" asked Butler.

"Oh, those were Catholics," said the reverend.

"Which makes it quite all right," I added. "The point is—if there is a point to all of this—that missionaries have a great political usefulness."

Tokyo

"Napoleon said that, not you," said Pectopah, with raised chin, still apparently posing for his historical oil.

"Then that makes it all the more true," I said.

There was a knock at the front door. The servant, who was standing in the corner, left the room.

"All of this talk gets us nowhere, in my opinion," said Pectopah, taking the final sip of his coffee and pretending to admire the cup. "Japan is great because she offers a haven for the white man's senses. It is the perfect place to be a male in our day and age, and I suspect that it will always be so. They can have the rest."

"Excuse me for interrupting, gentlemen," said the reverend, "but I failed to mention to Mr. Hearn that there was another special guest coming specifically to meet him."

I threw the reverend a hostile look which, I hoped, expressed some of my loathing for his reverential kindness. Would the man of the cloth please understand that I did not relish meeting these pathetic drooling sycophants!

"This man has helped us greatly in the procuring of construction materials for our new church. He says that he is an old friend of yours."

At the words "old friend" I turned toward the doorway to see Akira Hosoi standing in it. For a moment we stared at each other in disbelief at how age had changed our faces, our hair, our postures—in my case, the decrepit slouch had come as much from sitting on the tatami as from the run of time—over the past thirteen years. The others in the room, including Mrs. Winter and the old servant, watched us, sensing the tension, as if some kind of wrestling match was about to begin. Akira and I walked toward each other at the same time. When we met we stretched out our left hands and clasped them together.

We left the Winters' house immediately afterward and walked through the streets of the residential district. Virtually each and every house had a Rising Sun displayed on its facade. At one corner many people were waiting in a line. They held little pieces of metal—belt buckles, old tools, parts of disused machines—in their hands. At the front of the line two soldiers were taking the pieces of metal and putting them in various piles, recording the names of the donors to the nation's war effort. Not far away several young girls were putting the finishing touches on a large rectangular bed of spring flowers, the leaves, stems and petals of which made up the picture of a battle scene.

"While I agree with you on the point of pride, Akira," I told him, "why must every last citizen give up his meager possessions?"

"That is precisely the point. It is the fire of patriotism burning inside each individual that is important. Sacrifice alone is the proof of loyalty. We Japanese are not content, as the Europeans are, with slogans and idealistic words."

"But monks are melting down ancient temple bells to make guns."

"Why should I have any sympathy for rotten monks?" he said, stepping up his pace and moving ahead of me.

I caught up with him at a street corner, where we decided to wait for a rickshaw to take us into the center of the city. Two young men with short-cropped hair stopped some ten feet away from us. The taller of the two noticed me and called the attention of his companion to me by tapping him on the shoulder. The companion shook his head and said, "No, forget it."

"You oughta do it," said the taller man.

"I said no. What if I lose? Shame would be brought onto the heads of all Japanese men."

"You won't lose. Take a look at him. He's no bigger than you. What in the hell kind of a white bastard is he anyway?"

Akira, craning his neck in all directions to find a rickshaw, had not taken much notice of the men. The taller of the two approached me.

Tokyo

"Listen. I want you to arm wrestle my friend here."

"Eh? Excuse me, please. I am waiting for a rickshaw," I said in Japanese.

"Rickshaw? Hey, Buntaro, hear that? The man said he's waiting for a rickshaw. I think you oughta do it. If you're man enough, you'll win, so what do you care, eh?"

"Please go away," I said.

"What did you say, eh? You tellin' me to go away? Why don't you get the hell out of here, eh? This is my country."

"I am a Japanese."

"Eh?"

"I said, I am a Japanese."

The man could not grasp this. He merely stood gaping at me. But I could see by the shaking of his head, back and forth, that his anger was rapidly mounting. Without warning, he pushed me quite hard on my shoulder, sending me reeling backward. I fell onto the dirt road, hitting my right ear against a stone that jutted out of it.

"Not worth the trouble," said the taller man, returning to his friend.

"I told you, you idiot. Why bother with them? They're just the sort of scum that we'll soon be rid of here. When they see how strong we are, they'll. . ."

The remainder of his words trailed off as the two of them turned the corner and disappeared. Akira looked down at me, offering his right hand. But I managed to get up by myself.

"There is no rickshaw in sight," he said.

"Oh."

"I am sure that one will pass if we wait long enough."

I took a white handkerchief from the sleeve of my kimono and touched it to my ear. A small drop of blood stained its center.

"Those louts," said Akira. "I wish they would go to China or Russia to fight instead of bringing the battles here. We need people like that, but, I must admit, they do not know how to contain themselves sometimes."

"Is that all you can say?"

"What do you mean?"

"Contain themselves? Is attacking foreign-looking people an aspect of not containing oneself?"

"Well, they are unused to playing the role of Japanese in the new Japan."

"Is Japan new?"

"Of course it is. I have not followed your books over the years, but I understand that you have written much about the old Japan. It does not exist anymore, not even in the imagination."

"Uh-huh."

"While I must apologize to you," said Akira, "for the behavior of my fellow Japanese, I also know deep inside me that I have more in common with them than I have, say, with you. I knew that by leaving them alone nothing serious would come of it. Had I interfered they might have severely attacked you or me."

"Why? I am a Japanese, am I not?"

"Being Japanese is not simply a matter of calling yourself one. I could call myself a monkey, but that would not change the fact that I am a man. How can you know, for instance, what it is like to sit by the river under the Nihonbashi Bridge after walking miles and miles from the northeast, to see the river as we see it, truly to feel the Japanese elements and experience them in a Japanese way? No amount of study can give a man that. You cannot partake of what we share, no matter how hard you strive, Mr. Hearn."

Tokyo

"It has been years since I have been called that. But, the thing I always liked about you, Akira, was that you were able to honor someone and yet not grovel at his feet all the while."

"From now on we will all be like that. Japanese will, from now on, look on as others grovel to us."

"I see," I said, hailing a rickshaw runner who happened to be coming our way down a slope. "So, all my striving these past years—what have I been doing it for, then?"

Akira too raised a hand. The runner quickened his pace and turned his vehicle on an angle toward us.

"You will have to answer that for yourself."

It was early evening when we arrived at the theater. Akira had bought two tickets. We stood in the spacious entry hall, taking off our shoes together with scores of others waiting in line to hand their shoes to the old man who placed them in cubbyholes against the wall.

"I had thought of you, Akira, as an educated rebel."

"I am that," he said. "We are now an entire nation of educated rebels. You are still back in Matsue in 1890, Mr. Hearn. Do you realize how many years have passed since then? Not a few years, not tens of years, hundreds. Hundreds of years. You have seen our port cities of Kobe, Yokohama and Tokyo. This is the real Japan."

"You are right. I am still in Matsue. But not in 1890. There is no timetable to my stay. I have seen the real Japan, Akira, and it is hidden behind colorful fans, the most delicate and thin rice-papered windows, and masks."

"We were hidden, it is true," he said, handing his shoes to the old attendant. "But we have emerged. Do not deny us that. If you do, we will have to prove it to you in other ways."

I handed my shoes to the man and followed Akira into the theater.

"I won't deny you that. But I have every right to deny it to myself."

We sat in seats located in the middle of the theater. The play, "Yoshitsune Senbon Zakura," had begun as all Kabuki plays did, with low-key, nearly inaudible banter. Members of the audience were still arriving, and those who were in their seats were eating, drinking, chatting to their neighbors or calling to acquaintances at the far ends of the hall.

"I cannot believe how much you have changed," I told him.

"And how little you have. . ."

I took his left hand in mine and grasped it.

"After my little brother died and my sister, well, left Matsue, I quit my teaching job. I went to Yokohama and, thanks to my command of English, I landed a position in an import-export enterprise. In time, I became its president and a Christian."

I was about to ask him "In what order?" but the drama on stage was unfolding with drumbeats signaling the coming of a tense moment, silencing the spectators. I looked around. A young mother, eyes fixed on the stage, was nursing an infant. A man stood, walked down his row, bowing politely and gesturing with a choppy hand movement to excuse himself. When he reached the aisle he hacked and coughed loudly, then deposited an enormous glob of phlegm on the red carpet, returning to his seat, once again excusing the intrusion with impeccable courtesy.

"These are the mikado's subjects, all of them, including me," I whispered to Akira. "But do not forget that many mikados in history have been the sons of concubines."

Akira spoke softly but firmly, without turning toward me.

"Do not insult the mikado!"

"It was not meant as an insult."

"No matter," he said, now looking me directly in my right eye, then shifting his gaze back and forth between it and my blind

Tokyo

left. "We must stop the Russian Empire from devouring China. Otherwise the world will never come to know how protective we feel about many others who are less fortunate and weaker than we are. We shall do this despite the cost. We Japanese do not consider the cost of those things which we must do. We act. Civilly. We always act civilly."

The drama was swelling toward a crest of emotion, and the audience, Akira included, was being drawn in to it. I was unaware of the silence that had fallen on everyone.

"You Japanese like crazes, that's all," I said. "Now it is a craze for war. Once you get this out of your system, you will be free again."

My voice had inadvertently rung out throughout the space. The actor on stage was cutting a climax pose and grimacing grotesquely at the spectators, who were transfixed on his hyperbolic expression. My head, turning back, forth and around, was the only thing moving amid the flat of Japanese faces. I hunched forward, so as to be as small as possible, and walked along the row, excusing myself as I went. I continued to walk like that, hunchbacked, up the aisle, through the foyer and into the entry hall.

"I would like my shoes now, please," I said to the old attendant.

"By all means, sir. Tag, please."

"Tag? I did not receive a tag."

"Ah, you must have, sir."

"Did I?"

I searched the sleeves of my kimono.

"All people who check their shoes are given a tag."

"I must have dropped it. Look, I can see my shoes there, in that hole. See them? They are bigger and more worn than anyone else's."

"Yes, I see those, sir. But, I regret that I am unable to give you any shoes without a tag."

"But, damn you, those are my shoes!" I said, speaking English for the first time.

"Forgive me, sir, but I only understand Japanese. This is our house rule. I am sure that you will find similar rules existing in all of the theaters of Tokyo. All Japanese obey the rules, sir. There can be no exception for an *ijin*. Do you understand that word, sir?"

He continued, but now spoke his language painfully, methodically, as if each word would somehow screw itself into the depths of my skull. "You . . . must . . . wait . . . wait—do you understand?—until all of the others . . . Japanese . . . have claimed their shoes. Do you understand me, sir?"

I returned to the foyer and sat down. I must have fallen asleep, for I was awakened by the sound of loud applause coming from the hall. Quickly I went behind one of the souvenir counters and crouched down. The audience began to appear in the foyer, Akira among them. I could see them filing out in neat rows, neither pushing nor shoving, to the last man and woman excusing themselves profusely when, by accident, a toe was trodden on or an elbow brushed. Each of them produced a shoe tag. The attendants—the old man was now joined by the three women who sold souvenirs—took the tags and ran the short distance to the cubbyholes, rushing back to people with their shoes.

All of the audience had gone. Through the glassed walls of the counter—and the colorful souvenirs, rice paper fans and masks before my eye—I could see that only one pair of shoes remained. The old attendant was looking around for their owner. The women returned to their souvenir counter. I stood up, bowed to them and went to the entry hall.

"Ah, there you are, sir. Here are your shoes. I owe you a humble apology for the inconvenience which you have been caused, sir. These are . . . Eh? Oh, here's the tag. It was inside the shoes all along. Sir, you must forgive us for the terrible inconvenience

Tokyo

you have been caused. I am very, very sorry. We eagerly await your patronage once again. Thank you very much, sir. You are so kind. Please continue to think well of us Japanese. We apologize humbly for the terrible inconvenience, we . . ."

The old man kept on talking—and, I am sure, bowing—until I was well out of earshot. It was nighttime, and I was on the Ginza, the most up-to-date symbol of what Akira had called the "new" Japan. No one noticed me, however, as I walked, mumbling to myself about people's dapper dress, the reflection of light from electric street lamps against the fresh brick, the way in which the moon, nearly full, was covered by a grimy sheet of cloud.

Yakumo Koizumi may as well not have been there.

I had come to hate the city of Tokyo, a well-dressed ditch. More and more I found my dreaded blue devils making visits upon me—Occidental demons invading my Japanese soul. I despised everything about the university, except for my students, though my greatest joy came in the one hour of peace on the rickshaw ride from my home to it.

Setsu had insisted that I buy a swallowtail coat and a plug hat to see the emperor when he came to the university. I froze outside waiting for him, for we were not permitted to wear overcoats in his presence. Such inane sacrifices were the only things in Japanese life that the remaining fragments of my Occidental personality, let alone my weak aging body, could not tolerate.

I refused to install a telephone at my home. This meant that the literary leeches, Occidental and Japanese alike, could not just stick to me and force me to speak. Letters from such were placed graciously, unopened, in my octagonal oak rubbish bin. Finally, it was the maze-like geography of the city that defeated those intrepid parasites who strove to observe their unwilling host in the flesh. Tokyo life did boast some advantages after all.

One day, however, a young, freckled, lanky blond American walked into my classroom unannounced.

"I was unable to reach you, so I thought I would just pop in," he said. "I do so highly value your writing, Mr. Koizumi, that I simply had to hear you give your lectures with my own two ears."

This, I interpreted, as an outrageous maneuver on the part of the university to force me out.

"Get the hell out of this room immediately," I told him, standing only inches away from him, though my eyeball barely came up to his collarbone.

"I did not mean . . ."

"I certainly do not care what you meant. Out! Weasel! Parasite! Out!"

"I must resign immediately," I told Setsu upon arriving home. "I will not see out the end of this year as the academics' fool."

For two or three weeks I was unable to function properly, anger overwhelming all other emotions. It was then that I first experienced shortness of breath and a grip of pain in my chest as if armor were inside it and a merciless hand were pushing it relentlessly against my heart. I coughed up blood as well. Setsu called for the doctor, who ordered me to bed. He told me that I had had a mild heart attack, aggravated by bronchitis, and that this had caused blood vessels in my throat to burst.

I held a small round red-lacquered mirror to my face, my futon covering the rest of my body up to my chin. Most of my hair had turned white, and my cheeks were caved in like little tea bowls. I could see the flesh peeling off my face, leaving only a manikin's skull. Disease, that normal state of man, had rendered my countenance finely supernatural. I had found what I had been searching for: my personal style, my own words for treating this world. Yet, as I stared for hours on end into the round mirror, I came to realize that my life had been a mere running-in-place exercise, as

Tokyo

inadequate and futile as a description of all creation by means of a string of prosaic comparative and superlative adjectives.

I had considered going back to America, despite the memories of starvation and begging. There had been an academic offer. It seemed as if I had always been going to a new place to teach the people there about the old ones I had been in. Kazuo, my dear little boy, was my main concern. I wanted him to know English. Yet, if I took him to America or England, he would lose all that was sensitive and delicate in him. If we stayed here, what would the future—given his mixed blood—hold for him? Boys were already throwing stones at him, cursing him for his different looks. In Japan, what he had inherited would never be taken as richness but always be seen as a raw, unidentifiable stain.

The news that Saint-Pierre, on my wonderful Martinique, had been totally wiped out, with in excess of thirty thousand dead, was another blow, as if the gods were deleting, one by one, every step of my past. Mount Pelée, which I had climbed, swimming across the freezing water of its crater lake, had erupted, burying the town in ash. Was the world, I wondered, inflicting deliberate wounds on itself to destroy all colorful records of the past, turning history a single irretrievable and blurred shade of grey?

In May of 1904 the students had invited me to join them on an overnight excursion to Hakone. I had recovered sufficiently from the attacks on me and was anxious to get into the open air. I even compromised my principles to the point of riding on a train with all of them, as this was part of their scheduled plan.

While we were in the wagon, a small group of them performed a pantomime, to the shock of the ordinary passengers present. In this pantomime, Hirota and his female friend, Emi Inagaki, who had come along though not a student, decked out as cowboy and cowgirl of the American Wild West, appeared to be riding in an open carriage on the backs of four hefty classmates. Four other young men formed two horses, pulling the nattily dressed couple along the aisle of the wagon. At the end, they all stood and, arm in arm, sang what was presumably a popular ditty.

> Things have changed since those times, some are up in "G"
> Others they are wand'rers but they all feel just like me
> They'd part with all they've got, could they once more walk
> With their best girl and have a twirl
> On the sidewalks of New York

"Did you like that, sir?" asked Hirota, coming up to me somewhat out of breath. "We chose it because it reminded us of you."

"I think that you are now, without the shadow of a doubt, the teachers and I, the pupil."

"But, *sensei*, you can teach us so much about Japan that we do not know."

The train lurched to one side, sending Hirota and his friend, Emi, into the lap of a stern-looking middle-aged lady in a kimono with a damask obi embellished in a cerulean blue *seikaiha* pattern of tranquil waves in the middle of the ocean, a symbol of ever-expanding good fortune.

That evening, before dinner, I sat in a leather-upholstered chair in a sitting room of the Fujiya Hotel in Miyanoshita. The creamy yellow lights lent the room a cozy yet eerie atmosphere. My students were around me, some sitting on the large Persian carpet at my feet. I started to tell them a story. As I spoke, we were joined by tourists, Occidental and Japanese alike.

> This takes place in the Province of Tango, in western Japan, in a wealthy household not far from the sea. It is a true story, for I heard it directly from the mouth of the wretched man's issue. A beautiful young bride was obliged to take care of her aging, withering mother-in-law. The mother-in-law, more than anything, enjoyed tormenting the bride. She despised her for her loveliness and her youth.
> One night it was clear to the old woman that she was going to die. So she instructed her son to summon his sweet bride, for

Tokyo

she wanted her at her side when the moment came. The son, of course, obeyed his mother in her every wish, as was invariably the custom in those traditional parts of Japan.
So the young bride entered the bed chamber and was told to kneel on the tatami by the dying woman's side. The old woman had barely the strength to breathe. She motioned to her son, who was kneeling behind his bride, to come to her. The son crawled to her and put his ear to his mother's foul-smelling mouth. He nodded once, showing that he understood her command, and propped her up, thus freeing her hands.
'Mother wants you to take your kimono off,' said the son to his beautiful young bride. The bride was, naturally, surprised, yet had no choice but to do as she was told by her husband. So, she pulled down the top half of the lovely pale-blue kimono. The mother nodded, indicating that this was correct.

I paused for a moment in my story. The room was now crowded with people, some of them hotel staff. One young boy was evidently a baker's apprentice, for he was dressed in a white smock and white hat, covered in flour and bits of dough, one of which had stuck to his right cheekbone.

The bride was forced to obey dutifully, for this was the custom in those regions of Japan at the time. 'I want to touch her soft breasts, if only once in my life,' said the old mother, a trickle of clear phlegm now dribbling out of her lips and down her chin. 'Come closer to me,' she said, wheezing her words out. The young bride moved her knees forward an inch or two, stopping when they could go no further. The old lady slowly stretched out her crooked hands... like this... trembling like dry winter's branches, until they touched, with open palms, the soft smooth warm breasts of the young bride. She cupped one hand over each breast and said 'Ahhhh.' At that single word she gasped her last breath... and passed on.

I looked around the room. The people were staring directly into my right eye, their own faces but shadows against the glowing backlight of the sitting room lamps.

But that was not the end of the story. In fact, it was only the beginning, for the strangest things happen. The old woman's gnarled hands would not let go of the soft little breasts, even though she herself had expired. Her arms cleanly severed at the wrists as she fell back like a stone, and those wretched hands remained glued on to the breasts as if by some superhuman force. The young bride and her husband tried as diligently as they could to pull them off, but this only increased the pretty bride's torment. A famous surgeon from Toyama-no-Etchu was called in. But he, alas, could do nothing for the woman.

And every night, at exactly two o'clock in the very darkest middle of the night, the wrinkled old hard hands would squeeze... and squ-eeee-ze... the two exquisite soft breasts, torturing the beautiful bride, until her own heart too gave out and she passed away. She was cremated with the two hands still attached to her body and buried in the family plot alongside her mother-in-law.

The next morning we left the hotel at an early hour on our hike up the mountain. The rising sun was illuminating the tops of the tall Japanese pine and cryptomeria. I took my students' hands and, all hands joined, we marched along a wide section of path at the foot of the mountain. I was experiencing one of the rare moments in my life when I felt a natural part of a group.

"Where are Hirota and Emi?" I asked, looking around.

"Oh, they go ahead," said one of the students.

We passed a statue of Jizo with his white bib on.

"The protector of the souls of dead children," I explained to them.

"Yes. We know, teacher," said the student.

We arrived at a plateau. It was nearing noon, and there was an enormous bed of cloud stretching far out from the edge of the mountain.

"We call that in English a sea of clouds," I told them, once they had assembled along the cliff's edge.

Tokyo

"In Japanese," said one of them, "we say a sea of cotton. It is like, well, a sea of cotton."

"It would be good," I mumbled to myself, "if the end of all of this nonsense could mean the beginning of some sense, wouldn't it?"

I looked at them. They had obviously not heard my words. I raised my voice.

"I have been fighting battles for the gods, but they are not listening to me. Ha! Ha! Ha!"

I made certain that my three distinct laughs echoed in the valley. But, alas, only silence came back to me. The students looked even more puzzled than before. Suddenly one of their number ran to us from another part of the cliff.

"Please come, *sensei*, quickly," he said in a very agitated tone. "Quickly, *sensei*!"

I followed him around a small clump of bushes to another open area. At the very edge of the cliff were two pairs of shoes placed neatly beside each other. I immediately recognized them as belonging to Hirota and his friend, Emi.

"Oh my God," I said.

The student who had come running crouched beside the shoes, nearly teetering off the edge himself, and took a small piece of paper out of one of them. I grabbed it from him. It read, in English, "All is But a Minute Flicker. . . ."

"Oh my God," I repeated.

The students stood behind me at a loss, as I was, for what to do. Gradually I felt myself becoming disoriented, faint.

"We have got . . . to . . . this is terrible . . . I should have . . . those are my words."

I sat on the ground by the shoes. The clouds had covered the sun and the valley was dappled in shadows. I heard the students saying, "*Sensei, sensei,*" the words coming to me in delayed whispers. I turned my head. The students had formed two rows, and from a grove beyond them Hirota and Emi came walking with shoulders slouched, holding unlighted red lanterns. They both wore white bibs and were smiling. I immediately stood up, knocking one of their shoes—and nearly myself—off the edge of the cliff.

That night at the hotel I refused to have supper with them. I had my meal, a traditional Japanese one, sent up to my room instead. I left it untouched, and smoked my way through supper. But even the pipe tasted foul, my own saliva, aloe-like, coming back to me from my stomach through the stem. I fell asleep in a large armchair, leaving one chopstick sticking straight up and down in a whole fish.

What was the drama in the great books I had read since childhood, those that, I would be the first to admit, had changed my life? The Russian poet Tyutcheff had written:

"Happy is he who has visited this world
During its fateful moments"

But what were fateful moments? I had read those books to find in them the intersection of love and death. Yet, though I had sought this point in my writing and relished its detailing in the lives of others, I had managed to bypass it in my own. I had lived my life without inspiring those few people around me whom I truly loved, neglecting them for an artifice. I had more often than not mistaken brooding for contemplation, mis-rendered a clever choice of words for soul. All of this had achieved recognition for me. But those fateful moments had eluded me. I had created a reality merely by rejecting other men's definitions of it. And, in the end, it was all, very gradually, ceasing to make a difference to me.

Tokyo

That summer saw a second excursion. Kazuo and I left Setsu with the other children to go to Yaidzu at the seashore. We stood in our small front garden as I looked toward the house with my hand enclosed over my little boy's fist. The reflection of the sun on the windows seemed brighter than the sun itself, but through it I could see, like an all-white photograph on glass, Setsu's face, pouting and cross, half-hidden by a frame. I smiled at her, hoping that this would cause her to alter her expression. Perhaps it did. I could not tell, for the sun on the window became even brighter, and I was compelled to turn my eye away.

It was an exceptionally beautiful and clear day. I did not once let go of my little boy's hand as we walked down the lane toward the main street where rickshaw runners often waited.

At the train station, while I was buying our tickets, I heard a man's voice calling from behind.

"Mr. Hearn, Mr. Hearn."

I turned to see Peter Butler, the American publisher, now accompanied by a woman of the most rotund proportions, a cathedral on pumps.

"Oh, is this Lafcadier Hearn?" she said, holding her palms to her cheeks. "My, my. Land sakes."

"That's right. Uh, Mr. Hearn, this is my wife, Bertha."

"How do you do?" she said, taking my limp hand in hers and squeezing it three or four times as if it were an udder. "And what a dear little boy you have. You both look so lovely in your kamona. Is that what you say? A lot of people like the girls in kamonas, but I think the boys look sweet too, don't you, Lafcadier?"

"Now, leave Mr. Hearn alone, Bertha. He is on his way somewhere."

"Oh, maybe he's going our way," she said. "Look, Peter, his ticket is for the same train as ours. We're going in the very same direction."

She was holding up my hand and cocking her head to read the Roman-lettered name of my destination.

"I suppose you've seen so many of them, though."

"So many of what?"

"You know. Kamonas," she said, letting go of my hand. "And it's not just that, but everything they do. It's so artistic!"

She had virtually squealed when saying "artistic," pronouncing its middle syllable like the word "cheese."

We entered our train, sitting opposite each other.

"Ah, will you look at that basket that little girl is carrying there," she said, pointing out the window. "With baskets like that, the good Lord only knows why they want to have a steelmaking industry. I love your stories, Lafcadier. Do you know, I have read all of your books. Uh-huh. In fact I was the one who told Peter about you in the first place, didn't I, Peter?"

"No, I don't remember it that way."

"Oh, you don't remember anything these days, dear. It's true, anyways. Ooh, do you mind if I call you Mr. Ko-i-zoomey? They're so, oh, what should I say, quaint—that's the word I was looking for—those Japanese names. Like everything else here. Like everything you write about it. Just exactly as it is. Everything I know about Japan I got from you, Mr. Ko-i-zoomey. So dainty and quaint."

I looked at Kazuo, who was fast asleep, his head resting against my shoulder. I put my index finger to my lips, indicating silence. Mrs. Butler shrugged her shoulders and smiled with hands against her puffy cheeks.

It was hot and muggy inside the wagon. I too must have dozed off, for the next thing I knew we were moving past paddy fields and farmhouses with thatched roofs. Mrs. Butler was staring out the window, shaking her head in wonder at everything before her. Her husband and Kazuo slept. I dozed off once again. This time

Tokyo

when I awoke, the two Americans were gone. Kazuo was sitting opposite me by the window.

"Father?"

"Yes," I said, wiping the beads of sweat off my brow with the sleeve of my kimono.

"I don't like those people. Are they the same as you?"

"You mean from my country?"

"What is 'country'?"

I squinted my eye at him, feeling for the first time the immense gap that existed between us, not only in age.

"I will explain it to you sometime. When it becomes necessary."

We arrived at the inn in the early evening. From the window of our room we could see many people preparing lanterns to be floated on the water. A maid announced herself and opened the sliding door. She entered, together with the wife of the proprietor, carrying a large tray with food on it. Another maid followed her with a second tray. They placed all of the dishes on the table, first in front of me, then in front of Kazuo. The meal was an attempt at Occidental food, with meat patties that had broken apart under their pasty brown sauce, a salad of grated cabbage and chopped parsley, stewed potatoes with raw onions and some other concoctions I could not bring myself to contemplate.

Kazuo began eating with great gusto, as I had forgotten to feed him since we had left home. As for me, I could not summon the interest to start. The wife of the proprietor and the two maids sat on their knees in the room, waiting for us to finish eating. I lit my yellowed meerschaum, puffing on it until Kazuo finished, then ordered the women to take the food away, which they did without displaying so much as a twinge of disappointment.

Not long after that, the two maids returned to lay out our futons. It was eight o'clock, Kazuo's bedtime, and I felt strangely exhausted. We said goodnight to each other, I kissed him on the forehead, and we closed our eyes. But the noise coming from the room next door prevented us from falling asleep. There seemed to be some sort of party in progress, its drunken participants shouting out jokes and grunting songs to the professional delight of the women brought in to be with them. Suddenly they broke into rhythmic clapping, as one of them sang a *naniwabushi* ballad which I myself knew. It was the story of Hidari Jingoro, the famous sculptor of Buddhist images who had lost his right arm and carved only with his left, relying on a one-sided artistic vision. As much as I was repelled by this clapping and singing, I could not stop myself from mouthing the words of the melody along with the man in the next room.

"Kazuo," I said to my son, turning toward him. "Would you like to go for a walk?"

"Yes, I would, father," he said.

We went down the stairs, each in a *yukata* provided by the inn, and walked barefoot on the beach toward the water. There were scores of people of all ages on the sand, chatting, drinking saké or simply gazing at the lanterns floating on the sea's glassy surface.

"Father, can you do something?"

"What is it?"

"Lift me up."

"But I am fifty four, Kazuo."

"Please?"

I put my hands on his waist and lifted him until our faces met. He laughed, as if I were tickling him. He felt much lighter to me than I had expected, and I started to run, holding him up like that in front of me.

"Are you happy now?" I asked him, kissing his cheek while running.

"Yes, father, I am."

Tokyo

My feet were sinking into the sand, and I faltered, falling on my side. Kazuo, lying beside me, was still laughing. He clung to me. His warm cheek pressed against my forearm.

"What is this, father?" he said, noticing that my *yukata* had opened at the front, exposing my thigh.

"These are three scars."

"Did a ghost do it?"

"No. My mother did this to me when I was four, just before she left me. This scar is for the Father, this one for the Son, and this one is for the Holy Ghost. I recall her telling me that as if it were yesterday. It is the only memory of her that I have, though perhaps it is of my own imagining."

"Then a ghost did do it," he said, standing and brushing the sand off his shins.

"I suppose you are right."

I sat up on the sand, with Kazuo towering above me. We watched the sea and the lanterns bobbing up and down on it.

"I'm sleepy," he said.

"You go back to the inn. Can you go all by yourself? It's that building over there, with all the windows lit up."

"Yes, father."

He turned around and headed for the inn. I kept my eye on him until he entered it, then took my *yukata* off, left it on the spot and, wearing only my *shita-obi*, dashed into the water. I swam with a consistent and strong stroke for some distance from the shore before stopping. I remained in the water there for a time, peering at the inn far away, the gibbous moon, that hump in the sky, hanging, as if on a hook, above the hundreds of lanterns, lit red, between me and the shore.

A young couple was standing over me. I opened my eyes and saw them. I was on the shore, half-naked, belly up. How many minutes or hours had passed? The two of them jumped back as I sat up, as if I had returned from the dead. I could not recall swimming to shore.

"Oh, thank goodness," said the man. They walked off, swinging their arms.

There was almost no one left on the beach now. Not a single lantern was to be seen on the water. Some of them had been washed ashore, torn to bits of red rice paper and stick. I put my hand over the three scars on my thigh, running my index finger along each one.

The moon had risen to the zenith now, a deformed globe precisely opposite the one protruding from my skull. This coincidence struck me as one of the most profound drama—this contrast of two so similar absolute and deformed shapes.

It was morning in early September, and I had slept much later than usual. There would be no time for me to prepare the notes for my lecture. I had nothing to tell my students in any case. Perhaps it would, I thought, be best just to sit on my desk and say nothing for an hour. It might turn out to be the most stimulating lecture of my tenure.

I called to Setsu several times, but she and the children had apparently gone out. I went downstairs and saw that she had left my breakfast on the kitchen table. I put a tea towel over the food and returned to the staircase. I was forced to stop, rest and catch my breath a number of times before reaching the top.

I was able to see the room objectively as never before. It was thoroughly disordered, with papers, books, loose notes and pipes strewn over every inch of floor and desk space. Until then I had found this disorder not only accessible, but comforting. I knew my way in and around it as a child does his toy box. The Japanese have the phrase *kanzen muketsu*, which means "absolute perfection." But I had thought up *kanzen yuketsu*, "absolute imperfec-

Tokyo

tion." This had been my ideal. But suddenly even this ideal made no sense to me at all, its neatly disarranged black and white specks and planes swimming before my eye. I felt dizzy and sat down on the landing, my legs stretched out weakly, like a rag doll's. Beside me was a magazine. I picked it up and stared at it for a long time without being able to decipher the words on its cover. Letter by letter I read it out. It was a copy of the *Atlantic Monthly* for June 1904 with its feature article "By Lafcadio Hearn (Yakumo Koizumi), The Foremost Interpreter of Japanese Life." I mouthed the word "interpreter," whispering it to myself like an incantation, but could not understand it for the life of me.

I wrapped some books in a large purple *furoshiki* cloth and carried them to the street. A rickshaw runner who had taken me to the university in the past recognized me immediately, put my *furoshiki* on the seat, helped me up and started the hour-long journey with a spirited gait.

When I arrived in my classroom, all of the students were present. They stood up and bowed to me. I placed the *furoshiki*, unopened, on a chair in the corner, put my wide-brimmed hat, companion of so many years and places, on the desk and leaned beside it. The students sat down in their seats.

"I am very glad to see you today. But I do not feel like giving a lecture. So, you may use the hour profitably by going to the library and reading any book by any author whose name I write on the blackboard."

I stood up and went to the blackboard, pausing for what must have been two or three minutes with my back to them.

"What is today?" I asked them, turning around.

At first no one answered. Finally Hirota said, "Monday, *sensei*."

"Thank you."

I turned once again to the blackboard and wrote the following:

Roger Pulvers

LESSON FOR MONDAY. BAUDELAIRE. ZOLA. POE.

I held the chalk over the empty space on the blackboard next to "POE." But my fingers began to shake and I let the chalk drop into the rack below.

"That will be all."

The students stood, bowed, and walked out. Hirota approached me.

"I am very sorry, sir, for the naughty prank I did at Hakone. We got the idea because we read your essay about double suicide. We do not know anything about that, really. Nobody knows now."

"Yes. I know," I said, smiling at him.

"Thank you, sir. Sayonara."

"Goodbye, Hirota."

He left, shutting the door behind him. I sat at my desk, opened the drawer and pulled out one of my swirl-grained dark English briars. I lit it, more intrigued now by the rising smoke in front of my face than pleased by its scent. Moments passed. I heard sounds coming from outside. I had heard such sounds many times before and knew instantly what was causing them.

A parade was in progress on the campus. I stood, breathing with some difficulty, and walked to the window. There, passing below the tall cherry tree, were students and teachers of the university formed into two straight lines. Some were grasping flags in their fists. One student, with head shaven clean like a monk's, held an effigy of a Russian soldier, a short sword, sticking out of its belly, flapping up and down as he brandished his effigy high in the air. I could clearly see Hirota among the students in the parade. He was marching like the others, in silence with a vacant expression on his face.

I sat down on the floor below the window, my hand raised and resting on the sill. I tried with all my might to recall the words I had written years before, while still living in Matsue, not

Tokyo

long after my arrival in Japan. They would not come back to me. Something about everything—time, space, people—being shadows and shadows cast by other shadows, coming and going, appearing and vanishing. But that something . . . Oh, what was it? Shapes? What *was* it? Was it the shadow-maker? Is it the presence of the shadow-maker himself, somewhere still in the heart of the shadows? Yes, perhaps it is.

Afterword

I am finished writing this down now, and I can see myself in two places at the same time.

In one, I am sitting, head cocked to the side, more slouched and round-shouldered than ever before, and looking exceedingly comical, if I do say so myself. I am poised below a window, my hand raised, like that of an eager little Irish boy on his first day of school in England, trying, with that lofty gesture alone, to please so many people.

In the other place I am at a desk, staring blankly at my beloved hat, the one which I took with me from New Orleans to Martinique, then back to America and across the ocean to Japan.

Both images of me exist simultaneously with all else that has been a part of them from their inception.

The miraculous thing about this is that, in both images, both of my eyes are open, and I see with unblemished clarity, as I must have once.

Outside the securely locked window is the cherry tree. And though it is the end of summer—not the spring that brings the blossoms—the very few buds nearest me, now forever beyond my reach, are in full bloom, in defiance of the season.

About the author

Author, playwright, theatre director and translator, Roger's novels include *The Death of Urashima Taro*, *General Yamashita's Treasure* and *The Honey and the Fires*. He has also published numerous works of nonfiction, including his autobiography, *The Unmaking of an American*.

Born in New York and raised in Los Angeles, he arrived in Japan in the summer of 1967. He taught Russian and Polish in Kyoto for five years, before going to Australia to lecture in Japanese at the Australian National University in Canberra.

Among his many published or produced translations are the works of Kenji Miyazawa, Hisashi Inoue, S. I. Witkiewicz, and Nikolai Gogol.

Roger's plays have been performed extensively in Australia, Japan and the U.S. He has twice directed at the Adelaide Festival of Arts; and in Japan has worked with such actors as Kyoko Kishida, Makoto Fujita and Akira Emoto. He was assistant director to Nagisa Oshima on "Merry Christmas, Mr. Lawrence," and won the Crystal Simorgh Prize for Best Script at the 27th Fajr International Film Festival in Tehran for "Ashita e no Yuigon." He was also awarded the Kenji Miyazawa Prize in 2008.

About the cover

Artist and illustrator Alice Pulvers was born in Tokyo and raised in Tokyo and Kyoto. Now living in Sydney, her covers and illustrations have appeared in books by ABC Books and Shueisha, and she has illustrated stories and articles for magazines and newspapers, such as *The Japan Times*.

Alice has exhibited at several galleries in Sydney and has painted a number of commissioned portraits. She works predominantly in gouache, and pen and ink.

Lightning Source UK Ltd.
Milton Keynes UK
UKOW051002121011

180203UK00001B/23/P